STRONGER

STRONGER

Courage, Hope & Humor
in My Life with John McCain

CINDY McCAIN

CROWN
FORUM

Published in the United States by Crown Forum, an imprint of Random House,
a division of Penguin Random House LLC, New York.

CROWN FORUM with colophon is a registered trademark of
Penguin Random House LLC.

Photograph credits are located on page 253.

Hardback ISBN 978-0-593-23688-8
Ebook ISBN 978-0-593-23689-5

Printed in the United States of America on acid-free paper

crownpublishing.com

2 4 6 8 9 7 5 3 1

First Edition

Book design by Susan Turner

To John, Meghan, Jack, Jimmy, and Bridget
For their love, inspiration, and guidance

CONTENTS

PREFACE

————— ∞∞∞ —————

My husband, John McCain, never viewed himself as larger than life—but he was. He believed in fighting for the good and never quitting, and he had more tenacity and resolve than anybody I ever met. Knowing his iron will, I shouldn't have been surprised when he announced one day in 2017 that he planned to attend a conference on international security in Lake Como, Italy.

John had been diagnosed with brain cancer just a few weeks earlier. A team of doctors had whisked him off for emergency surgery and removed a tumor the size of an egg. They told him that he couldn't go to the conference. Flying was too dangerous. The change in air pressure could essentially cause his brain to explode.

But this was John McCain. He was going.

Our grown-up children begged me to convince him to stay home, but I knew I couldn't change his mind. Over more than three decades of marriage, I had learned that John would do what he thought was right and important no matter what anyone said. I also couldn't let him go alone. So a few weeks later, I got on the private plane with him, toting various medicines and emergency numbers in my carry-on bag. I stared at him intently as we took off.

"What are you looking at?" he asked.

"I've never seen a brain explode," I said. "I'm wondering how much of a mess it will be."

"Don't worry. I packed the dustbuster," John said, cracking the wry smile I knew so well.

People think that the main lessons I took from John were about honor, courage, and integrity. I did learn all that. But I also loved him for his humor, for the example he set on how to laugh even when the world doesn't seem to be going your way. He believed in staying optimistic, taking action, and never wasting time on anger. When he lost his temper—which did happen—he was quick to apologize, make amends, and move on. Like John, I can accept a lot and stay stoic when necessary. But I know there comes a time to stand up for yourself, too.

John survived the trip, head and brain intact. He made a big impact at Lake Como, so I'm glad he went. With his military background and deep understanding of world events, he had the respect of world leaders who listened to his views. He knew that sharing his perspective was particularly important, now that a new administration had taken over in America that displayed only the most naïve views of international policy. He spoke to the gathered leaders about the importance of allies, about his hope that America, despite the tone its new president had set, would stay committed in the world, rise to the challenge, and remain a beacon for the basic values of equality on which the country was built.

John's purposeful integrity was needed more than ever, but within a few months of that conference, his cancer progressed so much that his body was weakened and his brilliant, active career was forced to wind down. We retreated to our ranch in northern Arizona, which had always been our hideaway for peace and comfort, tucked amidst

twenty acres of woods and creeks. John loved watching the hawks
that soared overhead. He admired their beauty and majesty, and,
pointing them out to visitors, he would describe them as his special
companions. We wanted to fill his last months with the gentle sounds
of birds and animals and rustling leaves.

I kept visitors to a minimum—just enough so that he could see
people and still feel engaged but not be exploited. A lot of press
wanted to know what was going on, and I heard that one tabloid
show had offered $250,000 for a photo of him. Fake hikers with tele-
photo lenses made their way into our neighbor's woods. Almost every
day, I heard the buzzing of camera drones flying overhead.

During his thirty-one years in the Senate, John was widely known
and admired, and I had gotten used to our very public life. I had the
advantage of great adventures with him—trips to foreign countries,
dinners at the White House, two runs for president, and the chance
to make a difference in the world. But I had also suffered the down-
side of a public life, including personal assaults and vicious lies about
my children. I tried to keep my dignity and not lower myself to the
level of the attackers. Above all else, I saw my job as the protector of
my family, and that included John. In his final days, the line between
public and private wasn't hard for me to draw. I told the caretaker
that this was private property. If he saw drones, he could shoot them
down.

We didn't have to resort to that, and by August we knew the end
was near. John's closest friends and longtime advisers came to be with
us, and most of the McCain children arrived except our son Jack, who
was serving in the U.S. Navy, stationed in Afghanistan. On a summer's afternoon, we all had lunch and listened to the music from
John's favorite Frank Sinatra playlist. Our doctor, who was also a
neighbor and friend, came into the kitchen where I was clearing up
lunch dishes and said to me, "Look, we're close."

I had been preparing for this moment for fourteen months—but

you are never really prepared to lose the person you love. I ran to
John's bedroom and, in a burst of panicked energy, I suddenly knew
where John would want to spend his final moments. I turned his hospital bed around and pushed it out onto the deck. As I did, the music
from John's playlist brought up the Frank Sinatra song "My Way"
and the lyrics washed over us:

> *I've lived a life that's full*
> *I've traveled each and every highway*
> *But more, much more than this,*
> *I did it my way*

Out on the grounds in front of us, one of the hawks flew across
the house, then flew back and settled on a branch not far from the
bedroom. I like to think that he and John exchanged a glance. Then
with the sun shining, the hawk looking on, and "I did it my way" filling the air, John drew his final breath.

I knew that people loved John McCain, the man who did everything
his own way. But I wasn't prepared for the outpouring of respect and
emotion that we witnessed over the next few days. My husband spent
a lifetime giving everything he had in the name of honor and country,
and he had touched many people with his example of decency and
values. His father and grandfather were military heroes, and he lived
by the military code of conduct that he believed in and put above his
own personal welfare. He had spent more than five years as a POW
in Vietnam, being beaten and tortured, and when he was given the
chance of an early release, he said no. It wasn't how things were done.

On that first late afternoon, I could barely make it to my closet to
put on my one black dress, so I was grateful for John's terrific and
long-serving staff who arranged for a hearse and a motorcade of

SUVs to begin my husband's final journey. As we headed up the long dirt road, I choked back more tears, knowing it was the last time John would be on his beloved land. When we got to the paved road, I was stunned to see that many people from the neighboring towns had come out and were standing at attention, hats off and saluting. I will never know how they heard the news. As we drove along Interstate 17, every overpass was filled with fire trucks sounding their horns and thousands of people holding American flags. Helicopters flew overhead and a sheriff's department joined us as an escort. Throngs of people greeted our arrival in Phoenix.

We remained in Phoenix, and I watched in gratitude as his staff oversaw the many details for a national farewell. The memorials began on August 29, when John lay in state at the Arizona State Capitol. Crowds of people came to see him and say goodbye on what would have been his eighty-second birthday. When we headed to a service at North Phoenix Baptist Church the next day, hundreds and hundreds of people lined both sides of the street. Students and administrators from the two high schools my children had attended— Xavier College Prep for the girls and Brophy College Prep for the boys—had come out to pay their respects. Our family was blown away by their loyalty and support. It was a scene that we'll never forget, and I bet the students won't, either.

An Air Force plane took us back to Washington. When we got to the airport, a contingent of military personnel and members of Congress waited for us, standing in 110-degree heat to pay their respects. The national response kept escalating. John lay in state at the U.S. Capitol Rotunda, and the crowds were so huge that the hours had to be extended. I remember leaning over John's casket as the hour got late, not wanting to leave him alone for the night. But he had plenty of company. Leaders from around the world came to say goodbye, and I had never seen such an enormous gathering of international press. I had gotten used to encountering a lot of reporters during the presidential races—but nothing like this. For many, John's farewell must have seemed like a valediction for the loss of America's proud and self-sacrificing leadership.

The funeral service at the Washington National Cathedral was beyond anything I could have imagined. The pews were filled with dignitaries from around the world and all the important stewards of American democracy, including military generals, senators, and three previous presidents. The current president, not invited to the service, tried to undermine the proceedings with petulance and pettiness— but we ignored it. A roster of important American leaders whom we cared about, including Presidents Bush, Clinton, and Obama, attended, as did former vice presidents. I started at one end of the row to shake hands with them, and as I looked down the row, felt almost dizzy realizing that the line went on and on.

John wanted his funeral to include only those who led with the same honest concern for the greater good that he championed. Presidents George W. Bush and Barack Obama offered tributes, invoking John as an exemplar of American values. Obama observed that our current politics is mean and petty and born of fear, but "John called on us to be bigger than that. He called on us to be better than that." John had hoped his funeral would stand as a reminder of the dignity and worth that politics held before it was hijacked by fractious self-interest. He would have been pleased at how clearly the message was sent.

In the days surrounding the funeral, embassies from around the world sent me huge books signed for John, and I discovered later that many countries declared a holiday so that people could watch the funeral. It was that big. I looked around and saw everyone I have known and respected in politics. The world was saying goodbye to a great leader, while many worried that the global respect he'd helped generate for America was forever lost. I shared the concern, but I also worried about the seven McCain children, always my first priority. I knew that if they saw me crack, they would, too. John's courage meant so much to the country and the world. I wanted to be an example of that. So I stayed strong for my country and my children—and for my husband, too. He would not have been happy with me if I had been a weepy mess.

After the funeral, reporters tried to get my view on the outrageous disrespect Donald Trump showed my husband in life and death. I tried to stay above the fray, but it is worth saying that I found his small-minded jealousy of John sad but not surprising. When Trump was young, he found an excuse not to serve in the military. Not everyone can be a hero—but most who aren't stand in awe of those who exhibit uncontested bravery and honor, or at least show them respect. Bombast cannot replace courage, and flailing and nastiness can never overwhelm true valor.

The funeral was such an assemblage of power that the guest list got scrutinized and questions emerged. Here are some answers. I made some decisions based on what I thought my husband would want. Sarah Palin, who had been John's vice presidential nominee in the 2008 race, did not attend because in the fourteen months that John had been sick, she never once spoke to him. He had put her on the political map, and she didn't even send him a note of good wishes when he was down. That is not someone you invite to a final farewell. Ivanka Trump and Jared Kushner attended the funeral. I vehemently disagree with Ivanka's father on many things, but John always taught me that it takes more energy to be mad than to simply move on. I don't know exactly why Ivanka and Jared wanted to be there. But I am hoping that they came for the reason I would think—that they mourned the loss of my husband.

General Jim Mattis and General John Kelly, who were both serving in the Trump administration, showed great kindness in the days surrounding the funeral. They joined me and my family as we quietly went to lay a wreath at the Vietnam Veterans Memorial, and they offered support as we buried John. At the Naval Academy, General Mattis gave me the flag off the casket and he had another for John's mother, Roberta McCain. I was impressed all over again by the way people like Generals Kelly and Mattis, who have been imbued with a military code, invariably display admirable honor when needed. I have learned to rely on such decency and rectitude. Both generals believe in service to higher principles, so I wasn't surprised when they soon left the Trump White House.

John is buried in the Naval Academy right next to his best friend, U.S. Navy admiral Chuck Larson, in a wonderful spot overlooking the Severn River. There's a field at the edge of the river where midshipmen play sports most afternoons and on the weekends. John must be so happy with all the laughter and cheering in the air. Crowds of people regularly swarm up the hill to visit him—so he is forever surrounded by the energy and spirit and pride of the Navy. I feel great comfort knowing that he is in a place filled with joy and purpose. Because for John, that's heaven.

PART ONE

Gaining My Strength

CHAPTER 1

———∞∞∞———

My Man in Hawaii

When I was in my early twenties, newly graduated from the University of Southern California, I decided I didn't want to get married. Most of the men I met seemed like boys—young and silly. I worked as a special ed teacher in Phoenix and I wanted to help people, not spend my time at parties where all the young men seemed more interested in drinking and showing off than doing something important with their lives. Maybe I was just traveling in the wrong circles, but marriage seemed like it would take me away from being serious and making the kind of difference I felt I made every time I stepped in the classroom.

Then, on a trip to Hawaii with my parents, I met John McCain. He was there as the naval liaison officer for a group of U.S. senators heading to China. President Nixon had made his famous trip to China just a few years earlier, so this was a politically charged mission, and the group, with John as escort, had stopped in Hawaii on a layover. We met at a cocktail reception, and he followed me around the hors d'oeuvre table. The room was packed with interesting people, but his quick wit and easy manner made me want to stay at his side and ignore everyone else. I didn't know anything about him or his heroic military history. I did know that he looked extremely handsome in his dress whites. When he invited me out for a drink, I discovered he was also smart and well read.

Is there such a thing as love at first sight? I went back home to Phoenix with my parents, and John went on to China, but we didn't stop thinking about each other. He managed to call me from China, which wasn't easy in those days. Shortly afterward, I got a bad case of bronchitis and ended up in the hospital. He called me at ten P.M. one night and I thanked him for the lovely bouquet of flowers he had sent. He said, "I'm so glad you like them." We talked a bit more and hung up. Only much later, after we were married, did I discover that the flowers had come from another John I knew. He took the credit. We laughed about that for years.

We began a long-distance relationship. We had no email in those days, and it always felt wonderful to get John's letters, which were soulful and thoughtful and often filled with funny details about his work travels. I went to Washington, D.C., a couple of times with my family since my dad often had business there, and John and I would get together for drinks and dinner. Each time we met, his intellect and his understanding of world events left me awed. Certainly none of the guys I'd dated in college had such maturity. The more we talked, the more I yearned to spend my whole life exploring the world with him. I was still insecure enough to wonder how such a worldly man could be interested in me—my own experiences seemed so limited in comparison—but John asked questions about my life and seemed eager to understand my background and experiences. He made sure that I felt like his equal. And it wasn't all serious conversations. He had a way of telling stories that kept me laughing. Being with him was simply fun. I never felt quite as happy as I did when he was around.

John was still in the Navy then and his work commitments kept him busy. When he finally came to Phoenix to visit me, I saw him in civilian clothes for the first time, rather than his slick Navy uniform. My mom was an elegant dresser and I always tried to emulate her classically tasteful and refined style. John arrived on my home turf in a pink Lacoste shirt and red-checked pants. I gulped and thought, *Oh my*. How could I date a man who dressed that way? But then I looked at his warm smile and expressive eyes, and his mismatched style didn't matter. I realized I had fully fallen for him. I liked being part of his life—and if it came right down to it, I could help with the whole clothes situation.

John had been such a celebrated POW that I was slightly embarrassed to admit that I hadn't previously known about him or his experiences being imprisoned and tortured for five years in Hanoi. He was careful about how he shared his stories with me—usually leavening the terrifying events with his own brand of humor. In part, he didn't want to scare me, but it was also intrinsic to John to keep a light touch and a positive view. It's the same outlook that helped him survive the unthinkable circumstances in the first place.

"I obviously didn't want to get shot down," he said one night when we talked about that terrible time, "and I never thought I'd be there that long, either. But I understood it all when I signed up." He and many of his friends were professional warriors, trained for any conditions. They had chosen a military career and knew the risks. He thought it was easier for them than for soldiers who had been drafted into the Army before being captured. Later on, when I met many of John's friends, I realized that they were indeed incredibly strong—able to move on with their lives despite the devastation they had faced.

I was awed that John had emerged from five years of beatings and torture with very few emotional scars. He tried to ignore the physical ones, too, but I sometimes ached for him, knowing he couldn't lift his arms over his head and that one of his arms was shorter than the other. He compensated for those difficulties so purposefully that it was often hard to tell anything was wrong. I knew that one of his knees had been badly mangled in Vietnam, and that after a series of operations when he got home, he was thrilled to be able to bend it ninety degrees. His energy level was so enormous that he could outrun and outwalk anybody. Half the time, I couldn't even keep up with him.

His refusal to be bitter amazed me. He wouldn't dwell on the hardships he had faced—instead focusing on what he wanted to accomplish next. I thought he was the most extraordinary man I had ever met.

After I had known John just a short time, I started to rethink my position on marriage. Some days I could hardly believe our mutual whirlwind of emotions. I was astounded that someone so amazing would be interested in me. I was also a bit naïve about the relationship John was ending with his wife, Carol. They had been married for just a couple of years when John was shot down over North Vietnam. He said that during those five years of captivity, he began to wonder if he had married for all the wrong reasons. When he got back home in 1973, a lot had changed in both their lives. It's often said that war takes many victims. John told me that he and Carol tried hard to reconnect in the years after he came home, but "you're a completely different human being when you come out." The marriages of many of the POWs John knew did dissolve, because the challenges were so overwhelming. John tried to pick up his marriage again, but by the time I met him in 1979, he was living with his mom most of the time. Given that the marriage was foundering well before I entered John's life, I never liked to think that I was the catalyst for their divorce—but I suppose our connection played a part in the final unraveling.

I felt very sorry for what was happening and I felt guilty, too. I had enormous respect for Carol, who had lived through his imprisonment with great dignity and made valiant efforts to keep her family strong. But life is complicated, and the whisperings and gossip that other people offer as explanations don't really hold. It broke my heart when I heard people snickering that John married me because he was having a midlife crisis. *Really?* I would think. *Is that all I am? The object of a midlife crisis?* Forty years later, here is what I know: I married the man who was the love of my life, and I believe I was the love of his life, too. We were good partners and a great married couple. It took me a little while to figure all that out, but John knew it from the beginning. You don't ignore love when it happens to you.

When we were dating, John seemed so worldly and sophisticated that when he asked my age, I added on a couple of years. I didn't know that he had also shaved a few years from his total, since he didn't want to scare me off. Only when we got our marriage license and saw it published in the local newspaper did we discover our eighteen-year age gap. We both stared at the small print in the newspaper in disbelief—and then burst out laughing.

"Are you okay with this?" John asked me.

"You haven't gotten any less handsome," I replied.

And that was it. We loved each other and didn't have to change who we were. We were connected enough that honesty would never hurt us—it would just make us stronger. It was a lesson that we both heeded for most of our marriage. The few times we forgot and tried to make ourselves look better by hiding something from the other, we both deeply regretted it.

We got married at the Arizona Biltmore Hotel, just a few minutes from my family's home in Phoenix. I wore a classic gown that made me feel like a princess, with a high neck and long sleeves and a cascading floor-length veil that settled over the flowing train. In his elegant white-tie tuxedo, John was a far cry from the man in the red-checked pants. His best man was William Cohen, the new Republican senator from Maine who would go on to become the secretary of defense under President Bill Clinton. As I walked down the aisle with my proud father at my side, I was thinking only of love and romance. I didn't realize that the men waiting at the altar represented what would soon be the best of American politics—maverick leaders crossing political lines for the good of the country.

The wedding was a gorgeous fantasy (as weddings tend to be), but once we brushed away the last crumbs of wedding cake and headed back to Washington, D.C., reality set in quickly. The first year of marriage is always a learning curve, but mine was huge. John and I had never lived together, and I had never lived on the East Coast. Every day seemed to bring some new adjustment.

We started in a condo apartment in Alexandria, Virginia, a pretty city with a central district known as Old Town that was founded in 1749 and was once the home of President George Washington. I enjoyed walking through the cobblestone streets and redbrick sidewalks of the village, gawking at the rows of historic townhouses. Eventually, I found one to buy. John was happy when we moved in. Enthralled by the history, I kept saying, "This is perfect!" Our home had once been a stop on the underground railroad as a safe haven for escaping slaves, and later it was part of the British Consulate. In less savory days, it had been a house of ill repute. One warm summer day, John and I were sitting outside on the stoop when an older African American man walked back and forth in front of the house and then stood for a long time looking up at one of the windows. Finally he strode over to us.

"I used to live here," he said.

"Really, sir? What did you do?" John asked.

"I played trumpet right in that window," he said, pointing upward. "I was the entertainment for the whorehouse."

John and I never used words like that, and I was too stunned to know what to say. But John politely wished him well, and when he walked away, we both started laughing so hard, we could barely talk.

"You found an interesting house for us to live in," John said, when we finally caught our breath again.

Interesting it was—but I'd always lived in the big open spaces of the West. Living in an East Coast townhouse attached by a wall to the residence next door made me slightly uncomfortable. I figured I could get used to having neighbors so close by, but I didn't think I would ever get accustomed to sharing my space with rats. Real rats. Hiking in the western deserts, I'd seen prairie dogs and horned toads and the occasional spiny lizard, but the small, scampering East Coast rats terrified me far more than any of them. I suppose you can get used to anything—but in my case, I'd gladly take a Gila monster over a rat any day. I was also used to sunshine, and while days of one-hundred-plus temperatures had seemed normal to me, East Coast snowstorms were not part of my experience. I'd never lived in snow. I'd never driven in it. The first time I tried to get the car out of the driveway on a snowy day, it skidded and ended up on a neighbor's lawn.

As I said, a huge learning curve.

Not long after we arrived in Washington, John invited a friend and the friend's new wife to come visit. I'd always been competent in the kitchen, so I expected that entertaining with John would be a lot of fun. I would have been less excited if I'd known John had promised his friend a lobster dinner. Being from Arizona, I didn't have much experience with either the eating or cooking of seafood. But John could make anything an adventure, so I felt optimistic when we set out that morning to the waterfront to buy fresh lobsters. John picked them out, along with a few other things, and we put the box in the back of the car. It rattled around as we drove home, but I didn't pay much attention. I spent the late afternoon setting a pretty table and finding a nice wine.

Shortly after our guests arrived, I put on a big pot of water to boil and reached into the box to get a lobster. I knew theoretically that our dinner would still be alive, but I didn't expect it to be wiggling. I yelped and dropped it—and as I jumped back, I accidentally tipped over the whole box. John and his friend rushed in and began crawling around on the floor, chasing the lobsters and trying to grab them. It was like a scene from a movie comedy—and it suddenly struck me as hysterically funny. Instead of being embarrassed at the mess I'd caused, I started laughing. The guys on the floor looked up at me in surprise and then they broke into gales of laughter, too. We somehow got dinner made, but more important, the high spirits continued all night.

Whenever I think of that evening, I start giggling all over again. If ever I'm obsessing about setting a table just right or peeking into the oven to see if the bread is rising properly (homemade bread is my only bragging right in the kitchen), I remind myself that while good food helps make a good party, a great attitude and a willingness to laugh are really the most important ingredients.

I didn't always have John with me to save the day. I remained shy and anxious about making friends, and a lot of the old Washington stalwarts seemed to keep their distance from me. They didn't know what to make of me, and a lot of people who had met Carol wanted to hate me. John half-joked that being young, blond, and attractive added up to three strikes against me. I did the best I could and tried to stay above the cattiness and gossip. I didn't condone the assumption that being a young wife meant I couldn't have a brain of my own. I figured that in time, people would come to respect me for myself.

I kept thinking about the stories my mother, Marguerite—who everyone called Smitty—had told me about the beginnings of her marriage. She met my dad while working as a volunteer at a hospital in the South during World War II. Jim Hensley was an officer in the U.S. Army Air Forces (USAAF) at the time, and he flew B-17s as a bombardier in an outfit called the Flying Fortresses. (When I was young and heard his stories, I loved the brave sound of that name.) On his thirteenth mission, he was shot down over the English Channel and wounded badly enough to be shipped back to the States. He ended up in a bed at the hospital where my mom was working.

My dad was always proud of his years in the military, and despite his success later as a businessman, he talked about his experiences flying as being the most formative of his life. When he first met John, he was a bit awed, and he tried to impress him by saying, "You know, I was shot down, too." In fact, my dad had been shot down three times and was awarded a Distinguished Flying Cross—and he liked to describe each incident in full detail. John, fortunately, was very fond of him, and respectful, too. Dad had married his high school girlfriend when they were both still teenagers, but they got divorced long before I was born. After recovering from his injuries, he proposed to my mom—and they got married in Memphis, Tennessee, in 1945.

My dad left the military soon after the wedding, and he whisked my mom off to start their lives together in Arizona. He had been born in Texas and raised in Arizona, and she was Southern gentility. When the train stopped in Tucson, she got off wearing white gloves, an elegant hat, and a gracefully billowing dress—hardly the best attire for a scorching summer day in a dusty western town. She stood on the train platform for a moment, as disoriented as if she had somehow been transported to a distant planet. "Honey, I wanted to get right back on that train and leave," she said, when she told me the story years later. "I thought, 'This is not my cup of tea.'"

I wasn't sure that Washington with its rats and snowstorms was my cup of tea, either. But my mother had taught me to stay strong and not let demanding times get you down. Instead of getting back on the train, she stayed with my dad in Arizona and worked in his office through the early turbulent years. Dad had grown up poor, but his Air Force experience gave him the courage to believe that with energy and determination, he could succeed at anything. (He and John were alike in that way.) He put up everything he owned and borrowed $10,000 to buy a small beer distributorship. Arizona was booming at that time. As the population grew, so did my dad's operation. He built that small company into the largest beer distributor in the West—and eventually one of the most successful in the whole country. The press often talked about my dad's wealth as if it had just fallen from the sky. It bothered me because I knew how hard he had worked—though I suppose the success did come on the wings of those B-17s.

The beer and liquor business had a reputation for being rough-and-tumble. My mom later told me that there were times when the mob tried to roll in—but they never touched our family business. My mom was a fierce defender of my father, and she never hesitated in standing up to tough guys. I decided that a bit of Southern gentility combined with a steel spine was a pretty good model for me to emulate.

If my own mother's example wasn't enough, I had the added pressure (and encouragement) of now being part of the long line of strong McCain women. And they were definitely strong. John told me that when he was a little boy in the 1940s, his intrepid mom drove him and his brother and sister across the country in an old Model A. His dad was already overseas, fighting in the war, and Roberta was responsible for relocating the family to Coronado, California, to be closer to his naval base. Roads weren't exactly great in those days, and facilities were minimal—there was no drive-through McDonald's for lunch stops and no Motel 6 to leave a light on for you. I can only imagine how daunting it would have been to handle three little children through long days and nights in unfamiliar places. But she did it without flinching. Her own mother and grandmother had been pioneer women who traveled and remained stoic under great adversity.

Given all that, how could I complain about a few rats?

As John's father rose through the Navy ranks to admiral, his mother gained a reputation as a terrific cook and a hostess who threw fabulous dinner parties. Her style and strength made her enormously influential within the Navy. With her husband gone for long stretches of time, her skill in running their family enabled him to move into highly politicized roles, including as the commander of U.S. forces fighting the Vietnam War. She was exposed to a lot of information she couldn't talk about outside the house, including how the war was progressing and where different troops might be stationed. Then her son was captured, and she endured five years of waking up every morning knowing he was a POW and having no idea whether he would survive. My sons also served in the military, and honestly, I don't know how she survived. I marvel at her unflinching attitude and fearless spirit. When John died, his mom was 106 years old and still going strong.

Roberta was always incredibly kind to me and happy to offer advice about the daily idiosyncrasies of Washington, D.C. She kept her dignity in every situation and gave me helpful hints about getting along. Before one summer outing, she mentioned a movie called *Protocol*, which starred Goldie Hawn as a cocktail waitress in the capital. Invited to a diplomatic barbecue, she shows up wearing shorts, T-shirt, and sneakers—and carrying a boom box.

"I'd never do what Goldie did," I assured John's mom.

"I know, dear. But do understand that a barbecue in the capital has a different dress code than elsewhere. It's khakis and a blue blazer for men and the equivalent for women."

Really, how do you know these things unless someone tells you?

In 1981, John's dad died suddenly from a heart attack when he and Roberta were coming home from Europe aboard a C-5, which is a huge military aircraft. John and I went to Andrews Air Force Base to meet them. I remember climbing into the airplane and then taking a long ladder to the second floor where Roberta was waiting. She had just lost her husband, but even at that moment, she remained stoic and unflappable. She continued in that way through the huge military funeral that followed, where thousands came out to pay their respects to a great hero. I thought of her often through John's illness and in the weeks after he passed. From her example, I knew what it meant to stay strong for others, even as your own heart is breaking. In the end, that's even more important than having the right clothes for a barbecue.

Feeling a little lonely during my first months in Washington, I decided to connect with other military families. I began attending events where I could meet people. Women have been part of the Navy since 1917 when Loretta Walsh enlisted, becoming the first woman (other than nurses) to serve in active duty in the U.S. armed forces. The law banning women from being on Navy ships was finally ruled unconstitutional in 1978—but it wasn't until 2016, when Defense Secretary Ash Carter began integrating women into all branches of service, that women could have unfettered military careers.

My first experience with women in the Navy was at the events held for wives. I went to my first function at the Washington Navy Yard with great anticipation, expecting some version of my college sorority. But the Navy in those days lived by a strict pecking order, with seating determined by your husband's rank. John was a captain, so I had a seat near the front. I was twenty-four, and all the women surrounding me were in their forties and fifties. Everybody else my age was sitting much farther back. Navy wives tend to be lovely women, and they show huge strength for themselves and their families when their husbands are gone for long stretches of time. But it's also a club, and I hadn't paid my dues. Some of the women were standoffish, while others asked pointed questions about my background and allegiance to the Navy. I had the feeling that they were trying to figure out if I really deserved to be Mrs. McCain.

I could understand why carrying the McCain name into a room full of Navy wives bought me a fair amount of squinty-eyed scrutiny. John's father and grandfather, John S. McCain, Jr., and John S. McCain, Sr., had both been highly decorated Navy admirals, and they remained famous in military circles as the first father-son pair ever to achieve that lofty rank. The warship USS *John S. McCain* was eventually launched in their honor (my John was added as a namesake shortly before his death), and John's dad earned both a Silver Star and a Bronze Star for his heroics in the submarine service during World War II.

The McCains were Navy royalty, which meant that in military terms, I was like Kate Middleton marrying the queen's grandson. Yes, my commoner's roots got a lot of scrutiny, but I was proud to be part of the noble institution. I loved all the military traditions, and it made me happy that Washington (at the time) was such a tradition-driven town. I quickly learned that the Marine Barracks on the corner of 8th and I streets was one of the oldest structures in Washington, built under the auspices of President Thomas Jefferson. When the British captured and burned down most of the city during the War of 1812, they let the barracks stand—reportedly out of respect for the bravery of the Marines. I thought often of that story. Even though John had joined a different service, it made me proud to realize that honor and bravery could be rewarded even in the midst of war and fury.

I didn't find myself at complete loose ends. Because John served as the Navy liaison to Congress, we got to know a lot of political families, including Joe and Jill Biden, who were the first couple to invite us to their home. On a Saturday morning, John and I drove to Delaware, and we pulled up in front of a big, rambling house that was both stately and pretty. Jill greeted us at the door and I liked her immediately—she was smart and funny and just a few years older than me. She also understood what it was to be the new blonde in town. All weekend, I watched her, admiring her ease at entertaining and her comfort with life in general. The house was busy with children and friends. Nothing seemed to faze her, and I liked how down-to-earth the whole family seemed.

A few years earlier, Joe had suffered the horrific tragedy of losing his first wife, Neilia, and baby daughter, Naomi, to a car accident. His two sons had survived with injuries, and Joe had dedicated himself to healing his family. When he married Jill four years later, they had a daughter, Ashley, together, and the whole family became infused with the love and positive outlook that Joe and Jill emanated. As our children were growing up, we got together as families, often at backyard picnics where Joe and John would laugh together so much it seemed like a comedy routine.

In 2015, Joe would suffer another tragic blow when his elder son, Beau, died of a brain tumor. When John was diagnosed with the same illness a couple of years later, Joe showed remarkable kindness to our family. Politicians are sometimes better at making public statements than private ones, but Joe was graciously deft at both. He quietly visited our daughter Meghan in New York very regularly, just to talk and comfort and offer empathy and understanding. He won her unbounded loyalty.

Our friendship lasted and strengthened, as did my admiration for the Bidens, and when Joe became the Democratic nominee for president in 2020, I knew the country needed him to revive the sense of civility and decency that had fallen off a cliff in the previous years. Joe and John were strong advocates of bipartisanship, and as the incumbent president spouted increasingly undemocratic rhetoric and disparaged those serving in the military, I realized he was putting the lives of my children—who continued to serve—at risk. I could either yell at the TV or do something constructive. I made the decision to endorse Joe.

Joe told the press about my endorsement before I publicly announced it. I got a kick out of that. Joe is just like John that way—when he has good news, he has to share it. I told the Biden campaign that I would do as much or as little as they wanted, and I ended up with a packed schedule, doing several interviews and television appearances every day. A lot of Republicans knew the party had deserted its values, and I thought I could help Republican women feel comfortable supporting Joe. I was surprised by the amazing impact I had in Arizona and felt good when the state went for Biden.

My Republican roots run deep and I haven't given up on the party. I hope it can regenerate itself and swing away from the disgrace it has become. Republicans in Arizona and elsewhere deserve better. The party fell in thrall to a snake-oil salesman. I prefer the gold standard of politics that I learned from John and Joe—that whether you win or lose, you do it honorably. I am glad that when I travel internationally now, I can once again be proud of our president.

Before his five-year ordeal as a prisoner in Hanoi, John expected that his entire career would be in the military. He wanted to follow his father and grandfather and make it three generations of admirals. Now, though, he knew that his post-POW physical limitations would keep him from getting the command he wanted. Just a year or so into our marriage, he came home from work and sat down with me for a momentous conversation.

"I thought I'd be in the Navy for life," he said, "but all signs are saying I should move on."

Recognizing how his situation had changed was difficult, but he wanted to deal honestly with his own potential. He had been offered a new naval command, but it didn't fit with his fighter pilot mentality. He realized that he needed different goals and ambitions.

Still, he worried how I would react. "You thought you were

marrying a naval aviator," he said. "Will you be disappointed if that's not who I am anymore?" he asked.

"I expected you'd be a naval aviator until you retired, and now you're retiring. It's just a little earlier than I'd expected," I said with a smile. "We'll revamp and regroup."

"You think we'll be okay doing something completely different?" he asked me.

"I'm excited for us to figure out what's next," I said.

In one of those odd moments of sad coincidence, John's retirement became effective right after his father died, on the same day the admiral was buried. When we discussed the many possibilities that might be in front of him, John concluded that the logical step after his military experiences would be to run for Congress. He didn't retire so he could have a political career. He retired—and politics was the next choice that found him.

CHAPTER 2

Knocking on Fourteen Thousand Doors

P eople always say that you never forget your first time. That's as true for political campaigns as it is for romance. John had spent his whole life believing in the importance of service, and he saw going into politics as one more way to contribute to his country. Once he decided to leave the military, we had several conversations about his plans, and it was clear that politics fascinated and excited him. While it was his idea to run for Congress, it was my idea where to run.

"Let's just go home and do it," I said.

For most people, declaring a home district isn't a problem—you seek a seat in the place where you live or where you grew up. But coming from a military family, John considered "home" to be towns and cities all over the world. All during his military career, he stayed constantly on the move.

For me, it was much simpler. When I said "Let's go home," I meant to Phoenix, Arizona, where I'd grown up and felt deep roots. John didn't need much convincing. Going to the place where one of us had strong ties simply made sense. I had tried never to complain while we lived in Washington, D.C., but I was excited to plant our own family roots in the desert soil. If we had children, I preferred to let them grow and flourish in the open spaces and sunshine of Arizona rather than the hothouse atmosphere of D.C.

I had continued working as a substitute teacher while we lived in Washington, but as we planned to move back to Phoenix, I took a role in my family's company as a member of the board. It didn't involve any day-to-day responsibilities, but I liked being part of the bigger vision and decision-making process. John, meanwhile, went to work for my dad's company as a public relations executive. He appreciated his position—but both he and my dad knew it was just a stopgap until some political path became clear.

The problem was that the four congressmen from our state were well loved and had held their seats a long time. Then something unexpected happened. We heard whispers that John Rhodes, the very respected minority leader of the House who had been in Congress for thirty years, was going to retire. Rhodes represented the First District, which at the time included much of metropolitan Phoenix. This was the area where I grew up and that always felt like home. I loved the sense of western openness coupled with the buzz of a city growing larger and more vibrant every year. Within a day or two, I had picked the perfect house and signed a contract. By the time Rhodes made his retirement official, all the pieces were in place. Phoenix was our official home, and John could run for Congress from the First District.

He wasn't the only Republican who wanted that seat. Three other candidates—all with more political experience—announced they would be running in the primary, and since it was a heavily Republican district, the primary winner would almost certainly take the whole thing. John's years as the congressional liaison meant he had a lot of friends in high places. He started getting endorsements and money. Even so, I knew we had an uphill climb.

In politics, the first race isn't just memorable—it's usually the toughest. Everything is new, voters don't know you, and you're con-stantly surprised by what's been thrown at you. But there's something to be said for innocence, and the sense of freshness also makes it fun and exciting. Though his opponents started fighting hard and dirty, John and I decided to go ahead in our own honest direction. It was the only thing we knew how to do. We would meet as many people as we could and let them get to know us.

On a bookshelf in my house, I keep a pair of bronzed shoes—but they didn't belong to any of our babies. They are men's size 8 oxfords with big holes in each sole, the actual pair that John wore as we traipsed up and down the streets every day of that hot summer, knocking on doors and ringing bells to introduce ourselves. John would be on one side of the street and I'd be on the other. I'd hear him saying "Hi, I'm John McCain, and I'm running for Congress," and on my side, I would say, "Hi, I'm Cindy McCain, and my hus-band, John, is across the street. We live in the neighborhood if you have any questions for us." We did that all day, every day, seven days a week. We knocked on 14,206 doors, and John got 14,000 votes. You'd have to say he got very good mileage out of that one pair of shoes.

As we persisted with our person-to-person campaign, the assaults from his opponents came hard and fast. Their main point of attack was that John was a carpetbagger. He wasn't from Phoenix. After hearing that charge enough times, John grew tired of it, and he even-tually snapped back.

"You know, I was part of the military, so I didn't have the luxury my opponents did of growing up in one place," he said during one debate. "In fact, the longest I lived anywhere was my five years as a POW at the Hanoi Hilton."

He said it as a fact, not looking for sympathy, but people were moved—and perhaps shocked—by its simple truth. Every time I heard him repeat some version of that line later, I felt a little tingle up my spine. John's background was different from most people's, and we had to make sure that his distinctive history led him to the great future he wanted and deserved. I thought John was the smartest one in the race, that his strong personality and deep knowledge of the issues could make him an important figure in Congress. He should win, I thought, because he was good. The more people talked to him, the more they would start to share that opinion.

I never was quite as tough as John, so the barbs that bounced off him sometimes pierced my thinner skin. I didn't like it when one or two of his opponents made the case that since my family ran a beer business, I must be an evil sinner. I understood that they wanted to appeal to the many Mormons in the district, but I was mortified to think that anything in my life could hurt John. I was particularly taken aback by the mean-spirited claim that our marriage had been a setup, arranged by John to further his own political career. Supposedly he had plotted it all out as a clever maneuver that set him up to move to Arizona and use my family's wealth and connections to run for Congress.

As the spouse of a politician, you become fair game for all sorts of gossip and innuendo—so I knew that the attack on our marriage came from vicious speculation rather than any substantive information. I also knew how angry John became every time he heard those nasty whisperings. But being young and a little insecure, I still had a twinge of fear that I wasn't worldly enough for John. Newspaper reporters described me as pretty, but I never saw myself that way. Like too many women, I felt vaguely inadequate and not quite up to the situation I was trying to handle. Could the gossip be right? As ridiculous as I knew it to be, I decided to ask John about the marriage rumors one night as we lay in bed.

"I married you because you're beautiful and wonderful and I love you," John said, pulling me closer. "But I really wish the other part was true."

"Why?" I asked, slightly bewildered.

"Because plotting all that would make me an excellent political strategist. And the truth is, I'm really not."

We both laughed, and I wrapped my arms around him. Only John McCain would claim political naïveté as proof of true love. Some people wouldn't consider that the most romantic proclamation. But to me, it really was.

Looking back now, I wonder why it is so difficult for young women to feel confident in themselves. I often wish I could merge the strength I've acquired now with the youthful energy I had then! I spent a lot of time doubting myself in those early days of marriage and worrying about how people saw me. The sad truth about judging yourself through others' eyes is that if you're feeling insecure, you take every negative comment as proof of your failings, but the positive opinions barely make a dent. All through the campaign, I worried about saying something wrong that reporters would exploit to hurt John, but I didn't give myself credit for the good decisions I made in helping John to launch his career in Phoenix. Psychology research shows that we give a lot more credence to negative comments than to positive ones. Five people can tell you that you look great, but if one person criticizes your haircut, you worry about it all day. I was definitely that way.

Both age and experience can help you start to change that negative self-judgment. It's taken many years, but I don't get knocked out by criticism anymore. I realize that everyone puts their own spin on the world—and yours is as valid as any other person's. It's often said that you can't change the events that occur; all you can change is your attitude and response to those events. And it's true. Even since John's death, I've learned more about the power of perspective. If someone in government or media makes a vicious comment about John's life, I can be devastated, angry, and hurt. Or I can try to evaluate their position fairly, remembering what I know about my husband's integrity, and learn what I can from the situation. Whatever happens, I've stopped letting myself be defined by another's gaze.

Later, when I had two daughters to raise, I was determined to give them a core of independence and self-assurance. Some viewers who have watched my elder daughter, Meghan McCain, on ABC's *The View* may think that I succeeded a little too well. She isn't afraid to speak up, and her voice is powerful and well considered. She never tries to hurt anyone, and in the current political climate, that is both brave and unusual.

The taunts and assaults John and I endured in that first campaign for Congress were painful at the time, and John lost his temper once or twice when he thought opponents were being overly personal or unfair. But calling your opponent a carpetbagger seems mild compared with the out-of-control rants and personal attacks of some of our current political leaders. I think John would be appalled by the lies and incivility we've all experienced in the past few years. The savage pummeling of private citizens, military heroes, and political opponents has been motivated by personal gain rather than any consideration of the greater good of the country.

As he got older, John questioned the personal ambition that propelled him in politics. "I wanted to be a public servant, but it was also a thrill to be part of the game," he told me. "Do you think that makes it less virtuous?"

"I think it makes it all the better to be passionate about what you do," I said.

"I'm not sure I could have done it otherwise," he said thoughtfully. "It was nice to think of myself playing a small part in America's great history."

"You played a bigger part than you probably realize," I said.

"I enjoyed every moment of it," he said with a smile.

Motivations for success are always complicated, and I admired his ability to be so self-reflective. Coming from a line of brave men, maybe he wanted to prove that he deserved his place in their legacy. But he would never compromise integrity for fame or power. He proceeded with strength and honesty through that first primary campaign, and his forthrightness shimmered. Watching him, I began to understand that "I did it my way" wasn't just a song he liked—it was a way of life. I was thrilled when he won the primary (his way), and as expected, went on to triumph as the Republican candidate in the general election.

Now that he was a congressman, his work would be in Washington. But we agreed that our base would remain in Phoenix. John wanted to spend as much time in Arizona as he could, to understand the local issues and be able to represent his constituents well—and we wanted to raise our children in the West. In those days, most couples moved to Washington when a spouse was elected to Congress, but I was ardent that the Phoenix plan would be for the best. In this case, I was very much like John—willing to veer off the standard path and do things my (or our) way.

Meghan was born in October 1984, a couple of weeks before John won his second election for Congress and Ronald Reagan won his second term as president. John had a warm relationship with the Reagans, and he was pleased when the incumbent nearly swept the electoral college, winning 49 of 50 states and garnering almost 59 percent of the popular vote. I was too pregnant to do much campaigning for John this time, but it didn't matter. John had an easy win. Two years later, when Arizona senator Barry Goldwater announced that he wouldn't run for reelection, John began planning for his next step.

Even in his first few years in Congress, before he won that Senate seat, political leaders were watching John and predicting his rapid rise. While many politicians have a narrow focus, John showed a formidable intelligence and a broad understanding of foreign policy. From early on, people in government wanted his opinion on Vietnam, but they also sought his ideas on military strategy in Central America, Russia, and the Middle East. John also had an almost palpable charisma—he could simply walk into a room and people would drift over to be in his orbit. It's exciting to be pegged as the up-and-comer. We started being included in events around the country that were a lot of fun—and beyond the scope of what a first- or second-term congressman might usually expect.

One day, we got invited to go on a private plane with Tip O'Neill, the craggy-faced Democrat from Boston who spent ten years as the powerful Speaker of the House. The flight wasn't long, but it still felt like a very big deal. When we boarded, we noticed name tags for where everyone should sit. I found mine near the front of the plane, and John was near the back with Tip. I didn't mind being on my own, and I was impressed that the venerable Tip O'Neill, the guy in charge of everything, wanted to spend time talking and exchanging stories with a brand-new Republican congressman.

Cynics might say that he simply wanted to figure out how much his party had to worry about this rising star. But Tip's interest and curiosity in John went well beyond political positioning. Though he ardently opposed Reagan's conservative social policies, Tip wanted to hear John's point of view on the controversial topics of the day like Social Security. He remained open to different perspectives and sought ways to compromise that would draw people together. I look upon that era of politics as almost a golden age—and I wish that today's members of Congress could remember that they all came to Washington for the same reason. The goal is to make the country better, not just advance their party's agenda or their own individual ambition. Tip ended up very keen on John, and even though the Speaker was much older, and from the opposing party, they became great friends.

I've always had a fondness for throwing parties, and my pleasure in hosting events gave me at least one entrée in Washington. In our Alexandria townhouse, which we kept as our Washington base, I regularly set an inviting atmosphere that let people gather, talk, and relax. I hoped that since my style was to be comfortably elegant but never showy or over-the-top, people would like to come and be with us.

When John won his second term in Congress, I decided to invite our Arizona supporters to Washington to celebrate Reagan's inauguration. I had the party planned well in advance. After the invitations went out, however, Walter Cronkite—still the evening anchor at CBS News—invited John to go to Vietnam with him to visit his old POW camp and see how the country and the people had changed. Vietnam didn't yet have a diplomatic relationship with the United States, so this was an important opening-up to America.

"I'm going to have to go," John told me apologetically.

"Of course you'll go," I said.

"What about the party? Should we cancel it?" John looked at me anxiously. He appreciated how supportive I was when he had to make a hard decision, but he was always wary of pushing too far.

"We'll have the party," I said confidently. "It won't be a problem. You go to Vietnam, and I'll give everyone a great time here."

The day of the inauguration was unbelievably cold—snow pelted down, there were bitter winds and subzero temperatures. The official presidential swearing-in ceremony had been moved inside, and medical advisers deemed the frigid weather so dangerous for spectators that the inaugural parade was canceled. The White House quoted medical and military authorities as saying that given the conditions, "flesh can freeze within five to ten minutes." That sounded like a setup for a horror movie rather than a festive party, but I had all these big-deal Washington people coming, and I didn't plan to give up on a good time.

In the late afternoon, some of our Arizona guests arrived, the women trembling from the cold in their open-toed shoes and little fur shrugs—proper garb for an Arizona winter, but not very helpful in our Snowmageddon. I gave everyone a warm welcome and an even warmer drink. The guests relaxed and had fun, and while the weather raged outside, the house stayed cozy with cheerful celebrating.

At the end of the party, when most people had left and just a few close friends lingered behind, the doorbell rang again. I couldn't imagine who it could be. When I opened the door, I saw what appeared to be the abominable snowman. A very tall man with a hood pulled over his head stood there totally covered in snow, as if he been rolling through large drifts.

"Hi, Cindy, sorry I'm late," he said. "My car spun out on the parkway, and I had to walk here."

I blinked and realized it was Morris Udall, the longtime Democratic congressman from Arizona. He had run for the presidential nomination in 1976 and lost to Jimmy Carter, but he remained a powerful figure in Washington. John admired him enormously and was pleased to be on the House Interior Committee, which Udall headed. I opened the door wide and welcomed Mo to come inside and defrost. Almost immediately, my usual insecurities kicked in, and I quickly warned him that he wouldn't have John's cheerful and smart banter for entertainment tonight.

"I should have let you know that John is in Vietnam with Walter Cronkite," I said apologetically.

"I know he is," Mo said. "I thought it would be nice to get to know you, too. Let's just talk."

For the next two hours or so, that's just what we did. He was charming and funny and self-deprecating, but also passionate about issues that affected Arizona and the bigger world. I kept thinking how impressive it was that despite the weather, this high-ranking member of the House had decided to come to a party at the home of a new congressman. Even when his car broke down, he hadn't backed off. "I guess I'll walk to the McCain house," he decided. His level of kindness and caring has stuck in my memory.

Sometime after that, John and I had the opportunity to join Udall and Barry Goldwater at a dinner with just a couple of staff members from each of their teams. Even though they were on opposite ends of the political spectrum, Mo and Barry were close friends, and their families had been connected for years. Being with them and hearing their stories was like witnessing the history of Arizona come to life. I sat and listened and marveled.

One story that particularly intrigued me took a long time to tell, and Mo and Barry batted it back and forth with the joy of participating in a prolonged tennis rally. The basic outline was that Mo's grandfather David Udall had moved to the Arizona Territory in the late nineteenth century to establish a Mormon religious community. The church preached polygamy at the time, and he had three wives and many children. The local government had already banned polygamy, but for various reasons couldn't convict him. So they got him thrown in jail over a land dispute, even though everyone knew the real problem was his unusual lifestyle.

The Wild West really was wild in those days, and hangings weren't uncommon. Mo's grandfather was saved from pioneer justice by Barry's grandfather Baron Goldwater—a respected merchant who posted his bail and got him out of jail. I think there was some coda about the wives being thrown in jail and Baron rescuing them, too. Mo's grandfather immediately left town for safety.

By that point in the dinner, I was paying less attention to the details of the stories than to the warm feeling of goodwill around the table. I realized how deeply we are all connected by history—and I gave a big laugh when I discovered that the person involved in the land dispute was the grandfather of George Romney, the former Michigan governor, and patriarch to what became another grand political family. Beyond feeling surprised at how interwoven our lives all were, I was struck by a deeper message of the story that Barry and Mo were spinning. They seemed to understand that every life in every generation has its difficulties and complications. We can attack one another for what we've done wrong or we can be big enough to offer help and hope and understanding. If we take the second path, the results can be life-affirming. I imagined Baron Goldwater looking down at our dinner table, proud that his action in letting David Udall go free had helped give rise to a future generation of leaders.

After that dinner, I went home and called my father. "You won't believe the stories I heard tonight!" I said.

"Go for it. I'm sitting down," he said.

Though his roots didn't go back as many generations, my dad had been part of Arizona when it was still a sparsely populated cowboy state where people came for new beginnings. Even when I was growing up, people still arrived looking for minerals and wealth while others ventured west just to gain access to land and be free. The lure of a fresh start still holds for some. You don't have to be escaping from something to crave the freedom of the West. Rather, like John and me, you just have to dream of the future you can make together in a new place.

There's a reason I called my dad that night to tell him about the dinner. I knew he would be interested in the historical tales about his home state—but just as important, my dad had always been my closest friend and mentor. He believed in my abilities and tried to make sure I did, too. Instead of treating me as a soft little girl, he insisted that I could become whatever I wanted. He got a high school diploma before becoming an officer in the U.S. Army Air Forces, but he never went to college. Despite that—or maybe because of it—he cared deeply about my education. When I went to USC, I became the first person in my family to get a college degree. Since he achieved such success in the demanding beer and liquor business, people assumed my dad was rough-and-tumble tough. But I always saw him as very gentle, and at my college graduation, his eyes glistened with tears and pride.

As an only child, I was particularly close to my parents, who were my great confidantes on all matters. Outside of them, I didn't have a lot of other people I could talk to about things. I stayed in touch with some of my girlfriends from college, but being with John—an older man, a congressman, a politician quickly gaining a national reputation—seemed to have put me in a completely different world. Not wanting anyone to see any weaknesses in me, I refrained from sharing stories that might have revealed my anxieties or inexperience. I had to be perfect for John—a feeling that would soon lead to terrible consequences.

John and I made many couples friends in Arizona. While we shared good times together, I never really became confidantes with the wives. Many of them were connected in Washington, and I wanted to avoid being part of that town's notorious rumor mill. Meanwhile, John's regular travel to Washington made me feel a little lonely. I missed our physical closeness and lively discussions. On our nightly phone calls, there was an awkwardness that never existed when we talked in person.

Still, I considered our being separated for work part of our life together, rather than a particular hardship. Some women I got to know in Phoenix expressed endless sympathy that I was so often left to handle home and children on my own. They would shake their heads when we talked at a moms group or playground and say, "I could never do that." But I always laughed and replied, "Of course you could." We all learn to handle the circumstances where we find ourselves—and any situation feels more manageable when you keep a positive outlook. I knew that John would return home every week

and offer all the hugs and conversation and loving support that I
wanted. I also started to think of his being in Congress as a kind of
deployment—which fortunately kept him closer to home than the
military kind. His political life was part of his continued service to his
country, and I would always support that.

While John concentrated on national events, I focused more and
more on our growing family. And grow it did. John Sidney McCain
IV, whom we called Jack, was born two years after Meghan. Then
James, aka Jimmy, followed in another two years.

"He's away so much—where are they coming from?" my mom
asked, with a half-joking shake of her head.

I could have told her that even though John and I spent many
days apart, we also knew how to enjoy being together.

People have said you need a flow chart to understand all the complicated relationships that define our family—but it's pretty simple.
There are seven McCain children. All love their father, and he loved
all of them. When John married his first wife, Carol, she was a single
mom and he adopted her two sons, Doug and Andy. Within a year
they had a daughter, Sidney. That the marriage ended in divorce puts
John in a league with half the other people in America, but he defied
expectations by staying close to all of them. He was very dedicated to
our brood—we had Meghan, Jack, and Jimmy together, then adopted
Bridget as an infant from Bangladesh.

By the time John and I got together, Doug and Andy were mostly
grown, finishing up high school and starting college. Given how
close I was to their age, I knew I would never be a parent figure to
them, and I didn't need to be. But I did have to figure out what our
relationship could be. Without any guidebook to follow, I did what
felt natural—and set out to be friends with them. I wanted them to
feel relaxed with me, to know that I loved their father and cared that
he remained happy. I'm sure I made mistakes as I muddled along, but
I never felt any harshness or hostility from them. We didn't have to

be the Brady Bunch, but I wanted to inspire a level of goodwill—and I'm proud to say it worked.

Not long after we got married, John suggested that we take Sidney with us on a vacation to Bermuda. As always, John made it fun. We stayed on the naval base and rode mopeds everywhere, with Sidney sitting close to John. She was so lovely and precious and well-mannered that I didn't have to try very hard—I could just enjoy our being together. I treasured watching the two of them play on the beach, father and daughter. She had been only nine months old when John became a POW, and barely six when he returned. But for the rest of her life, she knew that she had a dad who loved her.

I grew close to Doug and Andy, too. They were kind and respectful to me, and I think they knew that I liked and admired them. I made the difficult decision when each of the boys got married not to attend the wedding. I'm sure people gossiped and made up stories about why I wasn't there—but it was really quite simple. I didn't want to make their mother uncomfortable. We had never met, and I didn't know how she would feel seeing me there. Wedding days are special. She deserved to enjoy every moment without distraction. I called each of the boys ahead of their big day and explained the decision. I told them that I loved them and supported them and wished them only joy. When Sidney got married, it was much easier. She eloped.

Andy graduated from Vanderbilt University in 1984, and a dozen years later, he raised the subject of coming to work for my family's business in Phoenix. He and his wife lived in Jacksonville, Florida, at the time, so it would be a big move. I cared that it be right for everyone. Andy interviewed with my dad, who gave a big thumbs-up—and I held my breath for a little bit after Andy came to Arizona. But he ended up loving the community, which loved him right back. After holding a number of executive positions at Hensley & Co., he became the company president in 2017.

·   ·   ·

John had just been elected to Congress when we got the invitation for our first White House dinner. We were thrilled to go. President Ronald Reagan had invited all the newly elected Republican members of the House, and it was a small class that year.

While I had been to many lovely parties with my parents over the years, I was awed the moment I walked into this one. Nancy Reagan had a flair for setting a scene, and she had the whole room gloriously lit with candlelight. The round tables glistened with the new White House china, and though the First Lady had been criticized for spending so much money on it, each piece was spectacular. The ivory china had a scarlet border with gold etched around the edges and a raised presidential seal in gold in the middle. As I looked at the expansive place settings, I felt a wave of gratitude that my parents had taught me the intricacies of silverware and finger bowls.

John had known Reagan prior to meeting me and had run an important campaign event for him in California. They greeted each other as old friends. As I watched them interact, I thought how perfectly John fit into this world. Our hard-fought campaign had been worth it. We had done it the right way and landed where we should be. When President Reagan shook my hand, my first thought was that he reminded me of my dad. His hand was large and gentle but strong. Just like my dad's.

Nancy Reagan hovered at her husband's side, and I immediately saw that her reputation for stylish glamour was well deserved. She looked beautiful in her floor-length red gown. The name cards showed John seated at President Reagan's table and me with the First Lady. As we took our seats, I complimented her on the gorgeous china, but she looked me up and down and offered only a chilly reply. Soon enough, she subtly let everyone at the table know that she was not a fan of mine. Every time I spoke, she glared at me like a judgmental parent. At one point, someone at the table said how exciting it must be for me to come to Washington and be part of Congress for the first time. I started to answer, but Mrs. Reagan jumped in first.

"She's not the one who won," she said abruptly. "Her husband did." Then she quickly moved the conversation in another direction.

I felt like all the wind had been knocked out of me. I never presented myself as anything other than a great supporter of my husband, but I understood the subtext. John's first wife, Carol, had worked on the Reagan campaign and gone on to run the East Wing of the White House. Mrs. Reagan had maintained a friendship with her and obviously felt great loyalty. That Mrs. Reagan herself was a second wife didn't make her any more sympathetic to my position. I'm not sure why she put me at her table rather than a different one. Maybe she wanted to find out what I was like. But she had no intention of accepting me.

I sat quietly and didn't say a word. In addition to advising me on which fork to use for fish and which for salad, my parents had taught me to always be polite. I certainly didn't intend to snipe back at the First Lady of the United States.

The grandeur of dining at the White House should have made for a magical evening. But I was young and terrified and made to feel uncomfortable. The act of surviving that evening stiffened my backbone and left me with one important lesson. When I left, I knew that however high John advanced in his political career, I would try to be kind to everyone. Nancy Reagan did great work in her life and offered passionate support for her husband in good times and bad. But that night always stood as a reminder to me that you should treat people with kindness no matter what the circumstances.

Not long after that dinner, I met George H. W. Bush, then Reagan's vice president, when he came to Arizona to speak at our Republican

Trunk and Tusk Club. (If the name sounds odd, just remember that Republicans are elephants!) John got a message that the vice president would like to see him after the event.

"I'm not going alone," John told me.

"Then I'll be your date," I said.

I wondered whether there was some special protocol I should know for meeting with a vice president—but it turned out to be a lot easier than I thought. The three of us sat down together and immediately launched into a fun and spirited conversation. Like so many people who met John, President Bush (as he later became) wanted to tell us about his own military experiences—and he had incredible stories. One of the youngest naval aviators during World War II, Bush gained a reputation for guts and daring, and his wartime exploits included several instances of remarkable heroism. During one mission when his aircraft was attacked and the engine caught on fire, he managed to bomb his target before parachuting from the plane. Landing in the water, he floated on a raft for hours before being rescued—and then he immediately joined the effort to save several other pilots whose planes had also been downed. For his bravery and heroism, he received the Distinguished Flying Cross.

"That's a great honor, sir," John said with admiration. "Congratulations."

"It's better than you realize," said Bush. He gave a furtive smile and explained that he had a specific reason for telling us the story.

"The person who pinned the medal on me was your grandfather," he explained.

John and I both stared at the vice president for a moment in incredulity.

"I can't believe that!" I said, meaning it only as an exclamation of surprise.

"Oh, it's true," said the vice president. Then he pulled out the paperwork he had brought along, showing that his award had been signed by John's grandfather, who had been an important admiral in the Navy at the time.

The story moved me beyond measure. The Bushes and McCains had both given years of service to their country, and that legacy of honor created an inextricable link through the generations.

A few years later, toward the end of the Reagan presidency, Vice President Bush announced that he wanted to succeed Reagan in the top job. After campaigning hard through the primaries, he won the Republican nomination. We went to New Orleans for the party convention and got caught up in all the hubbub and excitement, including many dinners and meetings with various decision makers in the party. A convention is always exhilarating, but this time I felt a hint of danger for John—and for me, too. As you start getting higher in visibility, the press comes after you, and it's their job to tear you down. My natural caution became even more acute, and I started to build a wall of wariness that I wouldn't let down for decades.

CHAPTER 3

A Full-Time Job

Being a political spouse can be close to a full-time job. One year, I spent a couple of months writing handwritten notes on thousands of Christmas cards that we sent to John's constituents. I liked connecting on a personal level with the people who supported John, and even small gestures like that made me feel part of a bigger purpose. However retro it sounds today, I didn't mind being John's greatest supporter. I explored the world, and met people who might never have otherwise been part of my orbit. Being with him didn't hold me back—it gave me flight, a courage I never would have felt on my own.

When home in Phoenix, though, I thought of myself as a normal mom whose goal was to give our kids a regular life. I drove carpools and participated in school activities and had my close friends as well as my mom-friends. Most of the time, people treated me like anybody else. Once in a while, though, I got a sharp reminder that people looked at me differently and paid a different level of attention to what I did.

Shortly before Christmas one year, I went out shopping and spent a happy hour or so browsing in a bookstore. John loved getting books as holiday gifts, so I bought some for him and others for the children. The next day, the newspaper published an itemized list of the books I had bought, along with a full description of where I had been, what I was wearing, and how long I'd spent in the store. I was astounded.

"I can't believe this. I feel so invaded," I said to one of my friends. "Why would anyone care what books I bought?"

She shrugged. "You're Cindy McCain, and the rest of us try to imagine what that's like. You must be used to that by now."

"I don't know if I'll ever get used to it," I said.

The experience left me deeply shaken. On my day of Christmas shopping, I'd had no idea that a reporter was following me. I hadn't purchased anything weird or salacious—just histories and biographies and children's books—which in a way made the whole experience even more disquieting. It was unnerving to think that my buying everyday books for my family qualified as news. If the mundane details of my life now merited interest, I knew we had reached a whole new level.

Like any mom, I felt protective of my kids. The bookstore incident made me just a little more cautious. We lived in a safe neighborhood in Phoenix, but now that I realized just how much we were scrutinized, I decided that my number one job was to protect my children from crazies, kidnappers, and attention seekers. The combination of John's power in the Senate and my family's financial position could make our children targets. Better for the children to complain about my overprotectiveness, I thought, than that something happen. I wouldn't let them go out bicycling by themselves or play without an adult around. Usually if they rode bikes, I rode right behind them.

As much as I fretted, I knew the limitations I put on the children were well balanced by advantages. We didn't go to Washington often, but when we visited there on school vacations or long weekends, John packed the time with fun and educational activities. We visited museums and monuments and military installations that gave the children a view of our country's history, and we had lighthearted moments playing ball on the National Mall. When John came home to Arizona, one of our favorite family experiences was marching in parades all over the state. At least, it was one of my favorites. The kids sometimes balked at the idea, but for John, parades were non-negotiable. He loved the pomp and pride that came with a parade, and it was the one time he insisted on showing off his family. We rarely asked the kids to do things outside their comfort zone, but a parade was a parade. John wouldn't hear another side.

"You're just walking with your family," I told Meghan when she hit an age where she thought it would be embarrassing to show up. "Nobody is asking you to play the tuba or twirl a baton."

She reluctantly came along—and at the end of the day, she had to agree that it had been fun. The kids and I always felt the elation of hearing the music, seeing the floats, and being part of something bigger than us.

Given how active and vigorous John appeared every day, I never thought about our difference in age. There was only one issue on which we had to deal with a generation gap. When I was pregnant with Meghan, I expected John to be with me at the birth, but most men his age were used to sitting in a waiting room and passing out cigars.

"Nope, you're going to be right there for the birth," I told him.

"In the delivery room?"

"In the delivery room," I said firmly. If he could handle a POW camp, he should be able to face his wife going through labor.

He was hesitant at first, and even more so when Meghan had to be delivered by C-section. But she was healthy and well, and he ended up thrilled with the experience. The next deliveries weren't quite so smooth. Jack arrived early, and John missed the delivery by a couple of hours because his plane coming back from overseas had been delayed. Barely two pounds, Jack was healthy but so tiny that he got whisked off to the NICU (neonatal intensive care unit) for a couple of weeks to gain some weight. I couldn't believe how small he was—his whole little body, from his neck to his bottom, fit in the palm of my hand. We finally brought him home in the tiniest Superman outfit you've ever seen. Despite his size, he was the happiest baby imaginable. We used to call him Happy Jack because he was such a cheerful little guy and never fussed. John claimed that he never even saw him cry about a wet diaper. He was the only infant I ever met who seemed calm and contemplative; he would sit agreeably all day in a chair if you let him.

Jimmy came along at a more normal six pounds, but the doctors could tell right away that there was a serious problem with his lungs. The extra amniotic fluid in a baby's lungs is usually cleared with the first few breaths, but Jimmy was in respiratory distress. His wet lungs kept him from breathing, and he was immediately hooked up to a ventilator. I was in my hospital room recovering from another C-section when John came in to tell me the devastating news. The doctors thought our baby might die. We had him baptized in the hospital because we weren't sure if he would ever come home with us. But the lung problem cleared and had no long-lasting effects. Jimmy was, and is, our active and outgoing guy. As he got older, he became the one who could make everything funny and entertain a crowd.

Even though I was the full-time parent with the children when they were growing up, John remained a fully devoted dad. When John was in Washington or traveling, we spoke at least once a day and often twice. Given his schedule, he usually called me, but I always had the comfort of knowing I could reach him.

"Put her through at all times," he told his assistants. "It doesn't matter who I'm meeting with."

If I had to talk to John about an issue with the kids, he was happy to let everything else wait. I never pestered him, but the kids knew that if we did call, their father would always stop what he was doing to talk to us. It's interesting how our biases about male and female roles affect our attitudes toward even the simplest things. Everyone assumed that John, a strong male, would put career first and leave children to me—so he got huge admiration from his colleagues and constituents whenever he prioritized home and family. I always wonder if a woman senator gets the same understanding when she takes a call from her spouse or child.

On weekends, John came home to Arizona and we did everything together as a family—we hiked, we camped, we fished, we played games. We bought a piece of property in northern Arizona that became our family retreat, and over the years, we expanded it in every direction, building new houses on the property and making it a comfortable oasis. The kids came up with their friends on weekends and got the kind of free-for-all playtime they couldn't have in the city. We had informal gatherings with people all the time, and a huge party with kids and grown-ups every summer. Paintball was a popular activity when the kids were growing up, and we organized wild paintball tournaments that encompassed the entire property. Everyone would run around hiding and ducking and shooting their paintball guns, loaded with capsules that left a nontoxic dye on the opponent.

One afternoon when we had broken into teams for a paintball tournament, I joined up with Sharon Harper, the mom next door who was also my close friend. We ducked and hid and played by the rules. But after a while, she and I both began to melt under the hot Arizona sun. Finally she turned to me and asked, "Are you tired of running?"

"Yeah, you bet," I said.

"Come on, I have an idea."

High up in one of the trees on the property was a very large treehouse, and so we climbed up and settled into it. What a luxury. We didn't have to run anymore and we could still play from our leafy perch. Sharon aimed her weapon over the side, and like a sniper, began picking off the other team's members as they ran by. We giggled, having as much fun from up high as the kids were having on the ground. Eventually, we were found out, and our technique prompted spirited outrage.

"Dad, tell Mom that wasn't fair!" insisted Meghan.

"There's no rule against it," John said.

"Well, there should be!"

She was right, of course. The rule was changed for future games so you couldn't climb a tree.

Outdoor adventures bonded our family together—and they often gave me a new view of John, too. John loved the beautiful vistas of Arizona, and he thought the best way to appreciate nature was sleeping outdoors. One year on his birthday, we headed off with Meghan, Jack, and Jimmy (we didn't have Bridget yet) for a camping trip. We had plenty of gear and, after a day of being outdoors, we found a lovely place to set up a campsite. I had waterproofed the tent before we set out, and now I unrolled the sleeping bags, pitched the tent, and got all our provisions ready for the night. Yes, all those were my jobs. John had many wonderful strengths, but handling practical details wasn't among them (and I say that in the most loving way).

We had dinner and a little birthday party for John, with the kids making s'mores and eating the birthday treats I had brought. When it was dark, we got the kids into the tent, and I lay down with Jimmy, the youngest, to make sure he got to sleep. Then John crawled into the tent.

"Do you want me to take over for a while?" he asked.

"Sure," I said. "That would be nice."

"Go sit by the campfire and enjoy the stars. You deserve it," John said.

Following his advice, I went back outside and lolled by the glowing embers, watching the sky get blacker and the stars get brighter. It was very quiet, with only the far-off sounds of some animals also enjoying the night. Then I heard another sound coming from the tent. I got up and crept closer and heard John singing very softly.

"Happy birthday to me. Happy birthday to me . . ." he crooned.

What was going on? We had already celebrated his birthday, so he couldn't be feeling forgotten. I opened the tent flap. Shining my flashlight in his direction, I saw a total mess everywhere. Little Jimmy had probably eaten too many birthday treats, and he'd thrown up all over John and the sleeping bags and everything in sight. As John tried to move around the small space, the situation just got worse. He had gotten Jimmy calm and was now just sitting there, resignedly singing his solo birthday ditty.

"Is Jimmy okay?" I asked.

"He's fine. Little kids throw up sometimes," John said.

I started to crawl into the tent, and John gave me his twinkling smile. The whole situation suddenly struck me as hysterically funny. I tried to keep a straight face and I saw John also biting back his laughter. We got the tent and the sleeping bags and the kids cleaned up as best we could. Then, when everyone had gone to sleep again, we went back outside. By now the campfire had completely died down, but the stars shone brighter than ever.

Birthday celebrations come in many forms, and as John and I looked back at that one over the years, it always made us smile and laugh. I remember that night with fondness for another reason, too. When John was running for president in 2000 and 2008, we met a lot of people who assumed that our lives were very different from theirs. It's true that John was a powerful senator, and I was (as the press liked to say) a beer heiress. But he was also the dad whose little kid threw up all over him on his birthday—and who handled it by singing himself a birthday ditty.

. . .

John had a vibrant relationship with all his children, and he didn't treat the boys and girls any differently. He had the same high expectations for all of them—though we all agreed that Meghan was his closest match in personality. We teased her for being John-in-a-skirt. And he in turn simply teased her because he could always guess how she would react.

When Meghan was in middle school, John told a funny story one night at dinner about some people from the meat lobby offering him a ride in the Wienermobile. Shaped like a hot dog on a bun, the Wienermobiles traveled the country to promote Oscar Mayer products. The amusing vehicles had been around for years, and the newest version was bigger than ever.

"Did you go for the ride?" Meghan asked.

"I told them I'd wait until I could use it to pick you up at school," John said.

"Never, never, never!" she roared.

John's plan to pick Meghan up in a Wienermobile became a running family joke. One day when Congress was in recess and John was in Phoenix, he heard that one of the Wienermobiles was nearby. He got in touch with the driver, and that afternoon, John and the Wienermobile showed up at the school gate. When Meghan came out, she was aghast.

"Daddy, how could you!"

"I promised you a ride in the Wienermobile, and here it is," he said jubilantly.

Fortunately, Meghan started to laugh. Even in those tender, vulnerable preteen years, she could appreciate her dad's pranks. They took a picture together in front of the frankfurter-shaped car, and from time to time now, she still looks at it fondly.

Whatever privilege they had when growing up, my kids developed a sense of honor and responsibility that outweighed everything else. They grew up to serve in the Marines, the Navy, the Army

National Guard, the Navy Reserve—and via marriage (Jack's wife) we can add the Air Force to our roster of family pride. Children can have financial comforts without an accompanying sense of entitlement, and I think how much better our country would be if more parents set the kind of example that John did of service and integrity.

Even kind and principled kids like mine can make their parents anxious during their teenage years. My fears of abduction continued after they outgrew their bicycles and entered the early driving stage. I always wanted to know where they were, what they were doing, and who their friends were. As Jack used to say, "Mom, you could have been in the FBI."

In the days before GPS was common, our family beverage company used tracking devices to monitor the routes of our delivery trucks—so I got a couple of them and put them on the bottom of the cars that the kids drove. I never told them about it, but if they were out some evening, I could watch a dot representing the car move across the screen. Usually the kids called me if they were going from one friend's house to another, and they almost never did anything wrong. But it still made me feel better.

I only ever caught one infraction. One night, Jack told me he was heading to a school event and instead went to a girl's house. Hardly the biggest disaster, but it revealed the problem with my plan to spy on my kids—the first time you complain, the game is up. I got around Jack's visit by staying vague and just alluding to what I might be worried about. When they were a little older, I finally confessed to the tracking devices, and the kids were astounded. It was about the only time that I outsmarted them.

Far more effective than the tracking, though, was the simple advice I gave each of them when they were teenagers: "Whatever decisions you make tonight, make sure they're good ones. Remember how it would look on the front page of *The New York Times*."

Thinking about your life in headlines is as good a deterrent for a teenager as any other. But for our kids, the exercise was more than theoretical. As their dad's political role grew more prominent, the possibility of their behavior being national news became all too real.

Meghan attended an all-girls Catholic high school because I thought it offered the best education. She did well in school, but when she decided to apply to Columbia University, the college adviser tried to stop her. She pointed out that not many students from the high school went to Ivy League colleges and even fewer to Columbia. "You'll never get in," the adviser said. "Don't even try."

Meghan came home and told me how discouraging the adviser had been. "What do you think I should do?" she asked.

"I think you should apply anyway," I said. "She's underestimating you."

"Then I'm not going to back down," Meghan said.

In true Meghan fashion, she went ahead and did everything she needed to do on her own. Meghan wasn't just smart; she had huge amounts of self-confidence and drive. Like John, she was endlessly tenacious. We didn't know a soul at Columbia, so she arranged for her own alumni interview, wrote her essays, and got good scores on her SATs. When she got accepted, Meghan was excited to be going to a top school and thrilled to be headed to New York City.

At that point, I hadn't spent much time in New York. I'd gone there for fundraisers and various other events, but I was unsophisticated about the city and still thought of it as dangerous and scary. When we flew there for her first day of school, I spent most of the trip thinking, *What am I doing?* It was just a year after the terrorist attacks of 9/11, with the trauma of seeing the World Trade Center towers fall still fresh in mind. Then, when Meghan and I went to check in to her dorm, I had to face another, very different trauma.

We got in line, and when we reached the front, a cheerful young guy greeted us. "Welcome to Columbia! Take anything you need."

"Thanks," Meghan said.

I noticed a big glass bowl sitting on the counter in front of him, and when I looked closer, I realized it was filled with . . . condoms.

As Meghan headed toward her room with her first bag of stuff, I called John in a panic and told him what had happened.

"What are we doing?" I said. "We can't leave her here."

"Settle down," he said soothingly. "It will be okay."

"Condoms on the counter, John, come on! Can't they at least take them away when the parents are still around?"

"Well, I guess it's better than not having any," John said.

"You make a good point. But I still wish they'd hide them from the parents!"

As Meghan progressed through college, I got to know New York better and stopped thinking of it as Sin City East. The Columbia campus is right in the city, but it's exquisitely beautiful and the perfect place to get a classic education. Columbia is one of the few schools that still require undergraduates to take courses in a core curriculum as a way of cultivating creative and intellectual curiosity. Meghan loved every minute of her four years, and, even though she didn't plan to make a career of it, she majored in art history.

The year after she graduated, she joined us on the campaign trail when John ran for president. We loved having her with us, and John appreciated the youthful, vibrant energy she brought. But it didn't keep him from continuing to tease her. At one town hall early in the campaign, John introduced Meghan and then turned to the crowd.

"Does anyone know of a job opening for an art history major?"

"Dad!" Meghan said, rolling her eyes.

But she laughed and gave him a little punch in the arm. She was way beyond the stage of being embarrassed by her father. Once you've driven with John McCain in a Wienermobile, the rest is a piece of cake.

. . .

My belief that being with John gave me flight turned out in one instance to be more than a metaphor. When John launched his first Senate run, we often took small planes to travel around the state. I tried to appear unfazed through the flights, but every noise and bump (and there are a lot of them on small planes) unnerved me. I couldn't admit it to anyone because I was surrounded on all sides by a flying family. My dad's early years as a pilot in the military were among the proudest of his life, and for John, soaring above the ground had been both his career and an everyday experience. I tried to swallow my anxieties, but I also knew I had to do something to quell my nerves.

It occurred to me that we are often most panicked by things we don't understand—whether on a grand political scale or a very personal one. A bang in the night might leave you drenched in sweat when you're home alone, until you realize it's just a raccoon encountering the garbage lid. Education in its many forms overcomes a lot of problems—so I decided the best way to feel comfortable on a plane was to learn what actually went on.

Without telling anyone, I signed up to take classes at ground school—the nonflying part of pilot training, where you learn about aircraft operations, how planes fly, and aerodynamics. I hoped that having some technical knowledge would help me stay calm. The instruction achieved that and a whole lot more, too. I found ground school so fascinating that I actually got excited about the intricacies of airplanes and wanted to learn more. Inspired, I went on to take weeks of flight training. Maybe I had the family flying gene, after all. One day when John arrived home from D.C., I told him to come with me, and I surprised him by taking him to an airfield and climbing into the pilot's seat of a small plane.

"You know how to fly?" he asked, in some combination of surprise and delight.

"I'd better, because we're about to take off," I said.

For much of that campaign, I flew John to his rallies and campaign stops, and it made him very happy. John had no issue about men and women being equal. He got to know my flight instructor, and she eventually became one of our full-time pilots.

I took great pleasure in flying—the realization that I could overcome my fears and be in control was as important as the simple fun of soaring around Arizona with John at my side. John trusted me completely. He often sat in the rear, but he never tried to be a back-seat driver. In fact, he would simply close his eyes and go to sleep. When I had a stroke years later, in 2004, it made me sad when the doctors said I shouldn't fly anymore. John, as always, tried to cheer me up with his teasing humor.

"I'm sorry you can't fly, because you were the best pilot I ever had," he said.

"Really? That's so nice of you," I said.

"The best because you were the cheapest," he said with an impish grin. "You were the only pilot I didn't have to pay."

In that first race for the Senate, John was leading in the polls from the beginning and, despite a few moments of anxiety, never really lost his edge. He won handily. In his Navy days, he had worked with and admired the influential leaders of the Senate. Now he was one of them. We should have been soaring high with or without a plane. But in just a couple of years, things would come crashing down all around us.

CHAPTER 4

Scandal

When you're young and starting out, it feels like everything happens at once—probably because it does. John began building his national profile and won his first three elections in the 1980s. During the same years, more or less, we had our first three children. In January 1987, I arrived in Washington with two babies in tow to watch him be sworn in as a senator for the first time. The next day, I planned to head home with the children, but John had a better idea.

"Let's have lunch in the Senate dining room," he said. "I haven't been there yet."

"Can we go with the babies?" I asked.

"Sure, why not?" he said. "It will be fun."

John could make anything fun, and his enthusiasm was usually contagious. We made our way to the dining room, which felt impressively clubby with lots of polished wood, white tablecloths, and blue leather chairs. Most of the senators back then were older men—in fact, at age fifty, John was one of the youngest—and the only woman was Nancy Kassebaum, a moderate Republican from Kansas. Having children around wasn't an everyday occurrence. It had probably been a long time since the dining room served its crab-cake sandwich to anyone under voting age. I quickly discovered that it had been even longer since anyone arrived holding bottles and babies.

"Could we get two high chairs, please?" I asked the maître d' when we walked in.

He looked at me as if I had demanded salt instead of sugar for my tea. Such a bizarre request! "I'm afraid we don't do that," he said.

"Maybe you could try," John said amiably.

"Yes, Senator, of course," he said.

They managed to dig up one high chair—but just one. We had a perfectly pleasant lunch, but with a baby and toddler doing what babies and toddlers do, not all of the food stayed on the table. I made some effort to keep things under control, but it was hard to do much about the mealtime mess around us.

One of the very proper waiters told me not to worry. "We don't get a lot of children in here," he whispered as he refilled my water glass. "We're all enjoying seeing some young blood."

When John was alone in Washington, he ate in the Senate dining room often, and he found it to be a good place for casual conversations with colleagues who held different political opinions. Many compromises in legislation were made over bowls of the signature bean soup, but I'm told that senators rarely have those informal meet-ups anymore. The spare moments in their schedules are taken up with fundraising visits and party caucus meetings, and the work of person-to-person legislating has fallen away.

As the senators spent time together in those days, so did their wives. By not moving to Washington, I missed being part of the whole ladies-who-lunch crowd. For the most part, the senators' wives were lovely women, and their weekly lunches revolved mostly around plotting good deeds—with some time for gossip, too. I admired the work they did in helping the Red Cross and other charitable organizations, but I was busy with a young family and not interested in the social scene. I was glad to be in Arizona, out of the limelight.

There were times, however, when my trips to D.C. required me to participate in activities with other senators' wives. I was never much good at small talk, but I found ways to be sociable and involved. Most of these women had worked just as hard as I did to get their spouses elected, but there were times when some of them seemed to forget that they weren't the official in office. One particular wife was known for always shouting at her husband's staff and demanding a limousine and private driver when the rest of us were going to an event on a bus. I wanted to say, "Really? Who do you think is the senator here?"

My early experiences in Washington influenced my feelings about it ever after. Like any company town, Washington can feel insular and hidebound—but it also has its own flavor, because most of the people got there by being tough and ambitious. I was happy to avoid the day-to-day interactions whenever I could. But I also recognized huge advantages to being a political spouse. I got a front-row seat to important moments in history, and I spent time with the people who shaped that history. You learn to accept the bad with the good. Almost always, it was a worthwhile trade.

My earliest glimpse of the ugly side of politics had occurred during John's very first congressional campaign when his opponents attacked my dad for being a beer wholesaler and referred to me as the beer heiress. It occurred to me that the higher you tried to rise, the uglier such attacks were likely to get. Sure enough, not long after John reached the Senate, he got enmeshed in the most painful political incident of his career.

The situation that the press eventually dubbed the Keating Five scandal revolved around the question of whether several senators, including John, tried to influence regulators to go easy on the Lincoln Savings and Loan Association, which eventually collapsed.

John's involvement grew out of a friendship he developed with Charles Keating, an Arizona developer and chairman of that savings and loan. Like John, Keating was a risk taker and a bold personality. In addition to the savings and loan, his Arizona-based businesses included real estate and shopping malls and hotels, and he loved to entertain. A former Navy pilot, he liked and admired John the moment he met him. Our families connected, too. When Meghan was a baby, we vacationed with the Keatings at their home at Cat Cay in the Bahamas and more than once flew there on Charles's private company jet. Much later, the press liked to dig up pictures of John enjoying some time off at Cat Cay in shorts and a baseball cap. For some reason, that photo of John enjoying himself in the Bahamas came to typify all that might be wrong with government. Even though we had avoided the shopping junkets, a personal trip had sullied his image.

Keating generously supported John's first campaign as well as the next two. He also contributed regularly to the senior senator from Arizona, Dennis DeConcini. Very shortly after John was elected to the Senate, DeConcini asked him and a few other senators to come to a meeting with Edwin Gray, the chairman of the Federal Home Loan Bank Board. They would be talking to Gray about federal regulations that affected Lincoln Savings and Loan Association, one of the companies Keating owned. Gray's team was already investigating whether Lincoln had violated some of the board's rules on investment practices. John was so new to the Senate, he didn't even have a permanent office yet. He hesitated at first, but Keating was a large employer in the state, and he felt some responsibility to know what was going on.

After the meeting he called me and said, "I might have just made a big mistake." His gut feeling that senators shouldn't talk to regulators didn't seem to be shared by anyone else at the meeting. Gray had explained that he wasn't directly involved with the Lincoln oversight, and he suggested that the senators meet directly with the regulators who were investigating Lincoln. He even offered to set up the meeting.

Eventually five senators went to that follow-up (and fateful) meeting. Along with John and DeConcini were Alan Cranston of California, Donald Riegle, Jr., of Michigan, and Ohio senator John Glenn, the former astronaut who in 1962 became the first American to orbit the Earth. Like my John, John Glenn was a paragon of courage who came to the Senate with a belief in patriotism and country. It often amazes me that a series of meetings could tarnish two great American heroes.

In the late 1980s, more than a thousand savings and loan associations began to collapse, and the government rushed in to make sure investors didn't lose their money. The problem had been building for several years, but by the end of 1989, a hugely expensive bailout was under way. The cost of the crisis has been estimated at $160 billion. The failure at Lincoln cost taxpayers more than $3 billion, and even though it was a small part of a much bigger problem, it became the symbol of a national fiasco.

The press whipped up a frenzy of outrage, and everyone began looking for a place to assign blame. Neil Bush, one of the sons of Vice President Bush, was caught up in the failure of a Colorado savings and loan that made headlines for a while, and he was quickly made a villain.

Pretty soon, John was caught up in the controversy as well. He was accused of urging the regulators to back off the Lincoln investigation—and his personal connection to Keating seemed to prove his motivation. The contributions Keating made to John's political campaign, and our trips on his airplane and visits to Cat Cays, were made to look like bribes. John and the other four senators had supposedly been enticed to intervene with the regulators based on the money they had received from Keating.

Financial upheavals have complicated roots. Focusing on a single event or on a name people know gives journalists a hook people can relate to. I sometimes think that the meeting of the five senators and the banking regulators was that kind of a target. After a reporter coined the phrase "the Keating Five" to refer to the senators at that meeting, everyone assumed that the failure of the Lincoln Savings and Loan had somehow ignited the entire crash, and the only reason it had failed was because the senators convinced the regulators to back off. The Senate Ethics Committee launched an investigation.

The day the hearings started, I walked in at John's side and immediately noticed the green draping on the tables. It looked like the setup at a military court-martial. I took a look at John's face and realized how devastated he was at having his honor and integrity challenged. *This is killing him and it's killing me, too*, I thought. A growing terror engulfed me as we each took our seat. I sat in the row behind John—the classic position of the unassuming wife desperately wanting to provide support. I felt so helpless to do anything, and that first day was just the start of weeks and weeks of torturous hearings to determine if the senators had been influenced to intervene by Keating's contributions.

I came every day, and sometimes I sat alone. People often say that you discover your real friends in times of trouble, and I realized how true that was. I've never forgotten the people who did sit with me. Many remain close friends to this day.

The senator in charge of the hearings, Howell Heflin, was a bombastic Southerner whom I'd never particularly liked, and his behavior virtually every day of the hearing made me physically nauseous. He was condescending, arrogant, and paternalistic in the most offensive way. "Is your little lady over there okay?" he asked once. Little lady? I was a senator's wife dealing with a major investigation. When a question came up later regarding an error I'd made in keeping records, he leered at me and got nasty, saying something like,

"Doesn't your little lady back there know the right thing to do?" The rude tone and vicious attitude compounded the anguish and pain I was already feeling. It shattered me. Heflin seemed the embodiment of a male attitude that a woman doesn't count as a person and can be ignored or discarded.

We don't always realize when our own confidence is being chipped away, but it happens to women every day—their self-esteem being nicked at by men who don't see them as equals, or from laws that say they can't control their own bodies and actions. A couple of years earlier, when I was in my midthirties, medical complications after the births of my three children led me to need a hysterectomy. While the procedure is much simpler today, it was a big surgery in those days—which made it scary and a little traumatic. Even if you know, as I did, that womanhood isn't defined by intact ovaries, you are losing a part of your body that has symbolic importance.

The doctors tried to be kind and soothing, but I remember lying on my back before the surgery with everyone talking over me, as if I weren't even there. John had stayed close by, chatting with the doctors about sports and politics, and I thought, *Well, all right now, can I put in a word here?* I had some questions, but what really appalled me was when John had to sign the paperwork giving permission for me to have the procedure. Shocking, isn't it? At the time, the husband had to sign the paperwork for a doctor to go ahead with a hysterectomy. Men have always tried to control all the details they can of women's reproduction, and this was one more egregious example. The need for a husband's approval fit in the old image of a husband owning his wife's body. What the woman wanted or needed didn't count.

I don't think I was fully aware how dramatically the whole permission issue diminished my sense of myself as a strong human being with my own worth. Subtle social messages tell women that we don't count or we're unworthy—and on some unconscious level, we start to believe it. The Senate hearing, and Heflin's condescending remarks, just made it all worse for me. By that point, the ethics committee had been looking into the Keating issue for almost two years, and senators who had nothing to do with the scandal were complaining about how drawn out the process had become. We learned later that an internal report recommended clearing John McCain and John Glenn and holding hearings on the other three. But the Democrats in control didn't want to give up on the one Republican they had on the docket—my John. So they dragged him into the public hearing, along with the other four.

One of the issues that emerged was the question of whether Keating had been giving out favors to senators, and our family's flying on his plane came up in that category. John always played by the rules, so we had paid Keating back for the flights. I knew we had done so, but I couldn't find the canceled checks that would prove it. The missing checks were fully and completely my fault. With John keeping busy and traveling so much, I had put myself in charge of the family finances, and now my careless record keeping had become a national issue. I was devastated. Years later, I found all the records and canceled checks in a closet in our house in Washington—but by then it was too late.

John kept telling me that the problem of missing checks wasn't as central to the scandal as I believed—but I thought he was just trying to be kind. I would have done anything to be able to stand up during the hearing and create the kind of climactic moment you see on *Law & Order*—to glare at Heflin and say *John is innocent, and I have the records to prove it!* Only I didn't have the records. My failure on that score ate away at my already diminishing self-esteem. In retrospect, John was probably right that those canceled checks might not have changed anything, since there were so many other complications around Keating's improprieties. But at the time, I blamed myself, as women too often do, for everything going askew. Almost immediately, I turned all household financial matters over to an accountant and never touched records again. But in the meantime, I felt terrified for John. I believed it was all my fault. My psychic pain became unbearable.

Physically, I also wasn't doing very well. After the hysterectomy, I had been in pain for a long time, and I filled the opioid prescriptions that the doctor kept giving me. Eventually, I didn't need them and switched to over-the-counter painkillers like Advil and Tylenol. Then a few months later, I went to Disneyland with the children. It should have been a fun time for everyone, but walking around with the baby in a back carrier, I blew out two discs. Not long before the hearings started, I had back surgery, which left me with postsurgical pain all over again. I went back on opioids.

With a positive outlook, you can get through any difficulties, but when you're feeling bad and negative, your gloomy perspective just makes any situation worse. And that's where I was as the hearings started—physically hurting, emotionally devastated, and at a low ebb of self-esteem. I started using the opioids more and more. I told myself that I needed them for the back pain, but the secret truth was that I couldn't face those hearings every day without some help. The drugs blurred our awful reality just enough that I could sit in the hearing room for hours and pretend to be calm—rather than wanting to run screaming from the room.

My experience with addiction is that it sneaks up on you. At first you have a reason for taking the drugs, as I did after the hysterectomy and the back surgery. But then the drugs begin to have such a powerful effect on your physical and mental state that it's hard to give them up. As I understand it, the opioids travel through the bloodstream to the brain and attach to receptors on the surface of certain neurons (or brain cells). The linkage leads to the release of dopamine, the hormone that causes feelings of pleasure. Your brain connects the drug to the positive reward, and when the good feeling wears off, various chemical reactions make you crave a new dose. We like to think we are in control of our actions, but physical addiction is difficult to handle on any conscious level. You know you shouldn't take more, but the signals from your body are very strong. If you've ever told yourself that you're going to take one bite from a chocolate bar and then devoured the whole thing, you know what it's like. And opioids are a lot stronger than chocolate.

When the hearings finally ended, John was cleared of all charges. The report basically said that he hadn't done anything wrong or violated any laws. John Glenn was also cleared while the other three senators—Cranston, Riegle, and DeConcini—were found to have acted improperly, with Cranston receiving a formal reprimand.

John's vindication didn't leave him feeling all that much better. He continued to hold himself accountable, saying that simply taking the meeting with the regulators had been wrong since it gave the appearance of influence seeking. But at least the dark cloud that hung over his head for a couple of years now dissipated. Everyone in Arizona, at least, accepted that he had done no wrong, and in the next election, he easily maintained his Senate seat. John Glenn won reelection, too, while the other three decided to leave the Senate.

While John's life in Washington returned to normal, mine continued spiraling downward as I returned to our family in Phoenix. Fully addicted to opioids and struggling with my own personal issues of self-esteem, I made another huge mistake: I didn't tell John what was happening to me. Like most addicts, I felt ashamed, and I did whatever I could to cover it up. When John came home, I always had the house running smoothly, and I maintained a carefully controlled front of conversation and good cheer. I don't think he ever had any suspicion of what was going on. Addiction to drugs is a cunning enemy. I knew I was in a deadly cycle, but I became very good at hiding the signs from anyone who could help me.

· · ·

Even as I felt my own world falling apart, I kept going with my daily activities. I stayed busy with my children and extended family and political responsibilities. Meanwhile, my desire to help people in need led me in a direction I never would have expected. I certainly never *planned* to start an organization to help people in dire circumstances around the world. But somehow the American Voluntary Medical Team evolved from a simple beginning—and grew.

It began when John and I went on a trip to Micronesia with a girlfriend of mine and her husband. My friend got injured and needed to visit the local emergency room. The conditions shocked us. Rats and cats scurried through filthy rooms, and the hospital's supplies were old and barely sanitary.

Fortunately, my friend emerged okay. But I couldn't forget the conditions I witnessed, and I wanted to do something about them. When I got home, I started collecting medical supplies. I scoured all our local hospitals and got whatever extra equipment they could scrounge up—and then shipped it to the hospital in Micronesia. It felt good to know I could make a difference, however small. Inspired by that feeling, I did the hospital run again. When the second round of supplies arrived in Micronesia, one of the people who headed the facility got in touch.

"We are grateful," he said. "But we also need doctors. Can you help?"

Well, could I? Why not. I put together a group of people I knew who were doctors and nurses, and we went off to Micronesia to see what we might do. The trip was exhilarating because I realized that yes, I could create change. With people in desperate straits, our simplest interventions could actually save lives. We treated one man whose arm was so badly injured that he would have died without one of our doctors there to treat him and stop the infection. In the labor rooms, I met women who expected to deliver babies while lying on mats on the floor and were incredibly grateful to have the clean beds we had sent.

Back home again, I started doing some research into the problems of global medical care. I saw that Micronesia wasn't alone—similarly terrible conditions existed in facilities around the world. I couldn't help everyone, but I had an idea for a mobile medical unit that would provide emergency care when and where it was most needed because of war or upheaval or natural disaster.

In launching AVMT, I got doctors and nurses involved and set up an administrative structure in Phoenix to oversee the projects. In the next few years, we went on dozens of missions, including to Vietnam, Bangladesh, and El Salvador. We ventured into Kuwait just a few days after the Gulf War ended in 1991. The missions were extraordinary. I felt moved and inspired by the strength of the medical personnel who gave up their own comforts, and sometimes risked their lives, all to help strangers caught in times of crisis. When people at home asked what we did, we often described it as a MASH unit. Everyone remembered the old TV comedy about the medical unit during the Korean War. While our feats weren't quite as funny, the circumstances were similarly urgent.

I am proud of the incredible missions AVMT undertook around the world, providing crucial assistance that changed lives. But my personal issues interfered again, casting a dark shadow over the organization I built. Addicts make huge mistakes that leave them ashamed, even as they might be having a positive effect in other ways. You know the old image of an angel on one shoulder and a devil on the other? My experience at the time was a bit like that. The medical supplies we had for distribution included prescription drugs, and I found a way to take some for myself. I won't try to offer any excuses or explanations—it was wrong. But remembering how helpless and needy I felt during that tumultuous time has made me aware of just how powerful addiction can be. Now that the opioid crisis in this country has reached devastating proportions, we have seen how easy it is for even the most moral and upright people to get caught in its iron grip.

Somehow my parents sensed trouble and decided to do something about it. They came over to my house one evening and sat me down in the living room. "Something is going on with you and we need to know what it is," my mother said.

I denied everything at first (as addicts do), but they knew me too well and pointed out all the ways that I wasn't acting like myself. No matter what happens, I'm usually on an even keel and don't get outwardly flustered. But my mother had noticed that I was more agitated than usual, getting excessively riled up for no obvious reason and experiencing what she described as "mild manic episodes." When John was around on weekends, I managed to control the episodes, but I saw my mother every day. I couldn't hide anymore.

"I need help," I said.

I told them about the opioids and my terror at being out of control. The moment I shared my problem, I felt something like relief. I was no longer completely alone, and I would have their support. But that didn't mean it was going to be easy.

"You've got to get off this stuff," my dad said bluntly. "Right now."

Looking at their anxious expressions, the depth of my trouble hit home. I thought, *Oh no, what have I done? And how can I make it end?* The potentially devastating consequences of my actions hit me hard.

"Right now," I agreed.

I went completely cold turkey. I got rid of all the prescription drugs in my house and called my parents whenever I felt on the verge of needing another dose. Somehow, I got through. I started to feel the cautious optimism that comes from surviving a dark time and seeing a hint of light on the other side. I don't mean to suggest that addiction can be overcome by willpower and determination, because it's far more complicated than that. But every day that I was back in control made the next day easier. Starting to feel clearheaded again, I was intent on putting that dreadful time behind me and moving forward.

When you're in the public eye, though, secrets have a way of not staying hidden for long. About a year and a half later, a vengeful former employee at AVMT raised an alarm about my earlier drug use. I knew the charge was going to get out, and I had no choice: I had to let John know the full story of what I'd done. We had a long and tearful conversation in which I shared all the details of my addiction.

I felt guilty about so much, but perhaps the worst was knowing that I'd failed to live up to the image of the perfect wife that I tried so hard to project. John saw it from the completely opposite view. He blamed himself for my problems and felt his own guilt for not having noticed the changes in me. Devastated by what I told him and hurt that I hadn't shared my burdens with him earlier, he let me know that I never had to put on a front for him.

"I'm here to love you and support you through any troubles," he said.

"I couldn't bear to think that I'd let you down," I said, tears streaming down my face.

We hugged and held each other. Then, he turned practical. He said that his main job now was making sure that I would be okay. In the following days, he got a lawyer involved. When an agent from the Drug Enforcement Agency came to question me, I told him that I'd made a mistake, admitted the extent of the problem, and took full responsibility. Now it was all even more likely to hit the press. John talked privately to some reporters, trying to get the bad publicity under control.

What happened to me next was about the worst thing you can do to somebody battling an addiction. Commentators on TV speculated whether John McCain had made a big mistake in marrying me. A cartoon appeared in *The Arizona Republic* about my drug use that was so vicious, it makes me shudder to this day when I think of it. Today, most of us understand that addiction is an illness. Back then, people ostracized me for being ill, and the public scrutiny and attacks were crippling. Absolutely crippling.

When something so overwhelming happens, you almost dissociate yourself from events. At times it felt like an out-of-body experience— I saw the cartoons and the TV clips and the articles, and it seemed like I must be watching someone else's story. But no—I was the one suffering the blows and sinking into a dark hole from which there didn't seem to be any escape.

One of the nastier attacks was the suggestion that I'd not entered "real recovery," since I had never officially gone into rehab. Even though I had been drug free for a while, I went to a fine rehab facility. I wanted to get out of the public view and show that I understood the seriousness of the situation. I am grateful now for the time I spent there, because it gave me a fuller appreciation that recovery is an ongoing process. One of the tricks is to understand that there *is* a future and there is hope. You make a point of looking for the positives. In my case, I reminded myself that I loved my family and they loved me. My marriage was real and strong, and my husband had been constant in his love and care. If I could just believe in myself and walk out with my head held high, I could resume life on a forward path.

With that new perspective, my depression slowly lifted. I emerged from that recovery period stronger—and with the sense once again that I could survive.

Depression and addiction affect so many people, particularly women, and I hope some of the shame and embarrassment is starting to fade. For decades, opioids and other prescription drugs were handed out far too casually. All you had to do was tell a doctor "My thumb hurts," and he'd send you home with a hundred pills. I won't blame the doctors' cavalier attitude toward women's conditions for my addiction, but it certainly didn't make anything easier. Early on, when I knew I needed help, I tentatively told my physician that I didn't feel right and could use his advice. Male doctors at that time had a tendency to attribute all of women's issues to anxiety—an update on the patriarchal diagnosis of "hysteria" that plagued earlier generations of women. Like so many male doctors, he didn't recognize that an upper-class woman could be abusing prescription drugs. Dismissing the clear signs that I was asking him for help to fight my addiction, he patted me on the shoulder and gave me a kindly smile. "You're a busy suburban mom," he said. "Go home and have a drink. That will help."

Good things can emerge from the worst situations. Up to that point, I'd had a very privileged life. The scandal made me aware of how easy it is for dangers and pitfalls to gut even the most perfectly structured existence. I had to talk about the addiction and deal with it—not just push it away. I also realized how easily our lives can be thrown off-balance. Sometime in my forties, I started to get regular migraine headaches, and they soon became so severe that I was admitted to the hospital several times for treatment. Nothing seemed to get them under control, and at one point when the pain was almost unbearable, the doctors started recommending opioids as the only treatment. I took them in the hospital under careful monitoring, but when I left, I was terrified that the opioids might lead me into another downward spiral. I admitted myself for another thirty-day treatment program, and mercifully, I got the support I needed to avoid another slide into despair.

The migraines continued to plague me for many years. It wasn't until 2010 or so that doctors at the Mayo Clinic got them under control by using the allergy drug Benadryl. People have individual responses to medications, but I was grateful to find something that worked for me. Eventually, the intense migraines diminished on their own. Chalk up one more advantage to getting older.

Illness is not a scandal, and it never should be. Almost every family I know has dealt with some kind of drug or alcohol problem, and new research suggests there may be a hereditary element to addiction. My father drank too much, but in those days it was treated as something funny to laugh about. John's dad also had a drinking issue, and while John may have acted like a typical kid around alcohol in his Naval Academy years, from the time I knew him, he went in the opposite direction. He stopped drinking nearly completely. He might have one drink a month, if it were a special occasion. And he kept that policy until the very end.

With the perspective of time, I no longer mind telling the story of my own addiction and recovery. We'd all like to change some things that we've done, but I think you need to accept the failures of the past to find the courage to move forward. Whether the past is clouded with addiction, depression, or some other problem, forward is the only direction we can head.

CHAPTER 5

Mudslinging Gets Everyone Dirty

W hen I first met John, he was the naval liaison to Congress, responsible for getting large congressional delegations (CODEL, in military-speak) to and from various countries on fact-finding missions. He had to manage passports, arrange for tickets, and generally handle all logistical details. Couples tend to split responsibilities, and once we were married, all those daily responsibilities within the family became my job. Looking back, I was amazed that he'd ever been able to handle that CODEL role—because the kids and I knew John McCain as the guy who was lucky if he could find his car keys.

John never fit neatly into a slot. He had his own views and eccentricities and was deeply allergic to groupthink. His originality made him an important senator, and it also made him an incredibly fun dad. He turned life into adventures filled with memorable stories. Every holiday season, we took a family trip to a place where John had a historical connection—and since his father and grandfather had both been stationed all over the world, we headed in all directions. John's delight in history made it fun for all of us—most of the time.

On one vacation when the older kids were in middle school, we traveled to Espiritu Santo, an island in the nation of Vanuatu in the southwestern Pacific. (It's east of Australia and west of Fiji, if that helps.) Espiritu Santo had been an important naval base during World War II, and John's dad and grandfather had both been stationed there. John enjoyed following his family's tracks. He also loved that the island had inspired James A. Michener's book *Tales from the South Pacific*—later adapted into the Rodgers and Hammerstein musical *South Pacific*. If you asked John his favorite book, he would usually reply *For Whom the Bell Tolls*, the brilliant war novel by Ernest Hemingway. But Michener and "South Pacific" were a close second.

On that trip, I was equally enthralled by the tropical island. We walked barefoot along the powdery white sands of Champagne Beach, where everyone—the locals and military personnel—had reportedly gathered on V-J Day back in 1945. They picked a glorious spot to look out on the gorgeous ocean and celebrate the Japanese surrender. The island also held a great mystery, since an old B-17 bomber had been found in its overgrown jungle a month or two before we came. We hiked up to see it, and John guessed that it had crashed long ago trying to land on an emergency runway.

Our kids were happy for the first few days, but it was a faraway island, and the lodgings were very different from the comfortable quarters we had at home. Most of the locals were subsistence farmers and we had rudimentary accommodations. I didn't mind. Traveling with AVMT, I had gotten used to camping out in tents—but the kids, particularly Meghan, had their limits. One evening we noticed some crabs scurrying toward our room.

"I guess dinner escaped from the kitchen," John said with a grin.

"That's not funny," said Meghan.

"Don't worry, we'll have something to eat," said John.

Meghan suddenly burst into tears. "I've had enough of this place!" she said.

John wouldn't let anybody stay unhappy for long. "Let me tell you a story about what happened here, and I bet you'll feel better," he said. The kids sat down around him, and John wove tales about the battles and bravery that had emanated from this small island. He talked about a ship that had hit a sea mine during the war, then he pointed to the glistening water and explained that the ship's remains were now just off the coast from where we sat. He described how his father and grandfather had seen each other on the island—the only time during the war that they had been together.

Meghan calmed down, and the boys were thrilled by the stories. We went off to a perfectly pleasant dinner with lots of fresh fruit and no crabs. Later that night, when the kids were asleep, I told John how impressed I was by his storytelling and his ability to keep the kids happy. "Michener has nothing on you," I told him. We snuggled into the slightly rickety bed, and as I started drifting off to sleep, I heard John humming softly. It took a moment, but then I recognized the tune from *South Pacific*.

"'Some Enchanted Evening,'" I said happily.

"That's how they all should be," he said.

In the Senate, John sometimes took positions that were at odds with those of his own party and sometimes even his closest friends. He stood his ground, but when he made mistakes, he owned up to them immediately and tried to fix them. I liked that about him. He was a person of his word, and there weren't—and aren't—many politicians like that. I learned on many occasions, though, that politics can bring out the brutal side of many people. Sometimes, that meant our family found ourselves in the crossfire.

In the year after we lost John, we were dealing with our grief and trying to come to terms with how we would go on without the husband and father we dearly loved. Trump's inexplicable attacks on

John's name and memory shocked all of us. This president who had never served in the military had previously sniped that John was "not a war hero." Now, months after John's death, Trump resumed his attacks, calling him "last in his class" and sneering, "I was never a fan of John McCain." John had wanted to repeal Obamacare if it were followed up with serious legislation to replace it. Since Trump had no plan to replace, John voted against leaving millions of Americans without healthcare. Instead of doing the real work of making policy, Trump just ranted about this "very dark stain against John McCain." Trump lives to be a bully, and it's easy to feel emboldened when someone is gone and can't respond.

At a speech in Ohio in March 2019, Trump went into a long rant against John, most of it either inaccurate or blatant lies. He claimed John had failed to pass a bill to expand services to veterans when, in fact, John had co-sponsored the bill and it is named after him. I never responded to the president's attacks because I didn't see any good that could come from joining in his war of words. As one of the hosts of ABC's *The View*, though, our daughter Meghan was expected to give her opinions daily (note the name of the show!), and I was proud that she spoke out forcefully. She tempered her much-deserved anger with a little humor, getting appreciative laughs when she said that her dad seemed to "live rent free" in the president's brain.

Before his death, John had been shocked by the disrespect Trump showed to people serving their country. As a candidate, Trump displayed cruelty and contempt toward the parents of Humayun Khan, an Army captain killed in Iraq. How could a commander in chief disrespect a Gold Star family? In his first year in office, he feuded with the widow of another fallen American soldier, Sergeant La David Johnson, who was killed in an ambush in Niger. Trump made a condolence call to his widow, Myeshia, in which, she said, he forgot her husband's name, and rudely said that Johnson "knew what he signed up for."

Our family soon realized that Trump's attacks on John were part of his bigger disdain for the military. My sons Jack and Jimmy grew up with a family legacy of service, and they believed strongly that the one solid thread in our country was support for the military. So our whole family was thrown into turmoil when we learned that Trump had referred to America's noble war dead as "losers" and called Marines who died in battle "suckers" for getting killed. He couldn't understand the concept of fighting for your country, and once said about those who volunteered, "I don't get it. What was in it for them?" Hearing the comments was frankly horrifying. I was concerned for my own children, who felt betrayed and angry, and one night, after yet another story emerged of Trump's corrosive insults, I went outside and cried. This was not the American leadership John believed in nor the one we raised our children to fight for.

It remains almost inconceivable to me that the commander in chief of the military would attack and undermine people whose children or loved ones died fighting for America. I know how painful it felt to have our family's grief met with brutality rather than comfort, and I can only extend my greatest sympathies to the other heroic families who found themselves similarly mistreated. Military and political families are often strong, but we are also human, and too many of us learned what it meant for there to be a complete absence of human kindness or appreciation for service emanating from the Oval Office.

When reporters called me for comments about Trump's disrespect for John and the military, I didn't reply. I remembered what John used to tell me—that if you get in a fight with a pig, you both get dirty, and the pig likes it. Many high-level military leaders have expressed their horror at Trump's behavior, and I obviously share their fury at having a leader so lacking in empathy and honor.

While criticism and disagreements are part of any political life, the only other time we experienced the kind of outrageous ad hominem attacks that Trump made his brand was during the 2000 presidential campaign. Unfortunately, fellow Republicans were once again responsible for causing us the pain—in this case supporters of George W. Bush. At the time, both John and Bush were seeking the Republican nomination for president. The Bush team chose our daughter Bridget as a target when trying to give Bush an edge in the South Carolina primary. Karl Rove, the ruthless campaign guru and later senior adviser to President Bush, has been named in press accounts as the mastermind behind this mean-spirited campaign. He has denied it, but I continue to believe he played an instrumental role in so viciously slandering John and Bridget.

Nine years earlier, I went on a humanitarian mission to Bangladesh and encountered Bridget as a tiny baby, struggling for her life in an orphanage run by Mother Teresa's congregation, the Missionaries of Charity. I took her home to Arizona, and when I stepped off the plane holding Bridget, I told John about the surgeries I had arranged for her to have nearby. We were holding a press conference, and he whispered to me, "Where is she going after the hospital?"

"I guess our house," I said.

He nodded. "I thought so."

We never had another discussion about it. She was our daughter from then on.

John's opponents, though, saw Bridget's physical difference as a way to play to voters' racial fears and worst instincts. John had achieved a big victory in the New Hampshire primary, and many pundits were already declaring that he would not only win the Republican nomination, but become the next president. John had stomped Bush once, and with polls saying we had a seventeen-point lead coming into South Carolina, it looked like it might happen again. With the bar to a Bush win set pretty high, the candidate's campaign decided to sink very low.

I was coming out of a McCain campaign event when I got wind

of what was happening. Flyers had been placed on all the cars with a distorted-looking picture of Bridget and the line "Did you know John McCain has a black love child?" The Bush supporters followed up with robocalls all through the state, asking voters the same question.

How do you respond to something like that? I tried to point out that our daughter was Bangladeshi and had been adopted—but John's enemies understood that innuendo can be more powerful than facts. In South Carolina, the divisions were strong, and the suggestion that John had an African American child unsettled some conservative voters. It was hard to know which part they thought was worse—the love child or the suggestion that she was black.

Stunningly, that completely fabricated attack caused our lead to slip. Once the Bush supporters saw that stirring up the rumor mill with dirt could have an effect, they continued with a vengeance. John's staff tried to protect me from some of the worst comments, and I was grateful for their efforts because I felt overwhelmed with hurt and anger. How could anyone involve an innocent child in their mudslinging? It was unfair and wrong. When John ultimately lost to Bush in South Carolina, I didn't get upset by the defeat—that's the chance you take in politics. But I was bitter about Bridget's treatment and always will be. Karl Rove never acknowledged his role in the campaign of lies and innuendo, but if he didn't start the attacks, he at least could have chosen to halt them if he wanted. He has never said he's sorry for any of it. I don't hold a lot of grudges, but I think one or two are well deserved.

Bridget was quite young during that campaign, and since social media hadn't yet taken over the world, she didn't know about the flyers, the robocalls, or how she was targeted. A few years later, when she was in middle school, she googled herself one day and came out of her room crying.

"Why does President Bush hate me?" she asked.

I swallowed hard, knowing I couldn't sugarcoat the story. I told her that President Bush didn't hate her, but that he and his campaign had made a mistake. I gave her an overview of what had occurred and tried to explain that she shouldn't take it personally.

"Dad and I tried so hard to stop it," I said. I left it at that, and told her she was a wonderful, kind, caring person whom we love dearly. But seeing her anguished face crushed me. That a child should have to ask why the president of the United States hates her simply broke my heart.

Starting that day and continuing to this one, I have explained to Bridget that she did nothing wrong and that while the meanness was directed at her, it wasn't really about her. John and I went on to have a warm and cordial relationship with the Bush family, and this incident became water under the bridge for us. But the fallout from a dirty campaign can have a lasting impact on a child, and Bridget has never forgiven Bush. She still wonders why the president of the United States didn't like her and why he attacked her simply because she was black. It horrifies me to realize that, on a less personal but equally devastating level, many children in America had to ask that same question during the Trump years.

Of all the political attacks we ever experienced, the South Carolina viciousness upset me the most. When I discussed it with John at the time, he tried to maintain some perspective. "Look, they're scared of us, that's why they're doing all this," he said. "Win or lose, they're scared of us. Please don't worry."

I did worry—and fret and fume—but I knew that I wasn't allowed to vent in public. I had to be a good political spouse. As a woman, you walk a really fine line, and if you put one toe over it, you risk being portrayed as the crazy, shrieking wife. When your child is a target, you're darned right you want to yell, and you want everyone to hear your outrage. But you have to control it. All you can do is take a deep breath and walk away. Or even better, you can spend your time developing what many of the senators' wives I knew reverentially called the Nancy Reagan Gaze—the look of devoted attention that the former First Lady fixed on her husband whenever they were in public. That expression—awed, admiring, and deferential all at the same time—became so famous that it got referenced on the First Lady's Wikipedia page. All of us were expected to display a similar devotion and near-perfect image. Perhaps Nancy had better training for the role because she had spent so many years as a Hollywood actress, and she knew how to play a part. (Meanwhile, she developed real power behind the scenes.)

I loved John dearly and felt proud to be at his side on a stage or platform when he gave a speech. I admired his words and the strength and humor he always showed. But part of the role of a political spouse is to laugh and smile at jokes you've heard a thousand times before, and to make it clear with your loyal gaze that there is no place else you'd rather be. Because I was a mom and not a trained actress, my mind sometimes drifted to my children at home, and I would yearn to give them a hug and hear what they had done that day at school. Other times, after standing for too long at John's side with the requisite perfect posture, I would feel a twinge in my back and want to kick off my high-heeled shoes and just lie down. But as a political wife, you never got to wiggle your toes.

There was one other scene from the South Carolina primary that I will never forget. The state is more diverse than New Hampshire. Depending on where you are, the views can range from liberal to far-right conservative. One Sunday I was attending a church service when the evangelical preacher began hollering from the pulpit on the evils of divorce and second marriage. He glared at me, and the congregants joined in giving me the evil eye. *So much for Christian love,* I thought. I felt desperately embarrassed sitting there, but I wanted to respect their religious views. I always thought that one advantage of campaigning was that I got to see other people's convictions—and I truly tried to learn and grow from every experience. But as I look back, I am struck by the likelihood that those same evangelicals who gave me side-eyed looks in the name of preaching purity later supported a thrice-married man who paid hush money to porn stars to cover up his marital infidelities. America is weakened when we choose to support religious rights only to discover that the sanctimony is just a mask for nasty political maneuvering.

I would have been devastated by lies spread about any of my children, but that Bridget was attacked seemed particularly egregious. She had been through so much from the day she was born and had struggled just to stay alive. I don't necessarily believe in destiny or fate, but it has always seemed to me that Bridget was meant to be our child—and she had picked us as her parents when she was just a few days old. I never told the details of the story on a campaign stage, but it was one of the central events in my life as a parent. The moments that led up to adopting Bridget forever changed my understanding of equality, women's opportunities, and hope.

In 1991, I went to Bangladesh with my AVMT medical team (our MASH unit) after a cyclone had caused widespread illness and injury. Longtime friends of mine from Arizona suggested that while we were there, we should visit an orphanage that had been started by Mother Teresa. After working hard all week to save victims of the cyclone, I decided to undertake a sideline mission on the weekend. I assembled a couple of doctors and some basic pediatric medications, and I said, "Let's go see if we can help the nuns."

The orphanage was located in Old Dhaka, and getting there turned out to be as complicated as navigating an Arab market—there were no addresses and you had to keep stopping and asking people the best approach. The narrow roads worked best for rickshaws, not cars, and the cyclone had made the conditions even worse. When we finally arrived at the orphanage and pulled up, we were horrified to see the body of a grown man lying across the gate. We rushed over to him and realized that he had recently passed away, possibly from the cholera epidemic spreading through the region. Not knowing what to do or where to go, the family had laid him in front of the orphanage. We called for help and, after some delay, continued with our mission.

The nuns welcomed us inside, and we confronted an amazing scene of 160 orphaned babies—all of them girls. In Bangladesh at the time, cruel gender stereotypes reigned, making girls so undesirable that parents abandoned them at orphanages. Neatly lined-up rows of cribs held the infants, and we saw another row of about thirty potty-chairs for the toddlers. The nuns were thrilled to see us, and we asked if we could help them.

"Yes, you can help," one of them said, "and if you can bring more supplies and doctors, we are grateful to have you anytime."

During our three weeks in Bangladesh, I went to the orphanage every Friday, Saturday, and Sunday. I played with many of the little girls, and the nuns steered me toward two infants, just a few weeks old, who were lying side by side. One had a heart condition and the other had a very serious cleft palate. The extensive surgeries they needed were beyond what our team could perform, and while the kind nuns were doing everything they could, they worried that the girls wouldn't survive.

"They're girls, so the government won't do anything for them," the head sister explained to me. "If you can get them out, they could be saved. But they won't get help here."

I looked at the beautiful, innocent babies and I understood the choice in front of me. I could leave them here to die—or I could try to bring them home to the United States. I didn't hesitate.

"We'll get them out and get them help," I told the sister. "The first step is that they need passports. Can you get those?"

I don't know what the nuns did or whom they bribed, but we got the passports quickly. I went to the U.S. Embassy to get the medical visas that would allow me to take them with me to the States. "I've got two babies I want to bring out for humanitarian purposes," I explained.

I had already spoken to the director of a hospital in Phoenix. He quickly jumped on board and lined up doctors and medical staff to take care of the babies. The arrangements were all set, and everyone was ready and excited. The day we were to leave Bangladesh, I drove over to the orphanage to pick up the two babies. A nurse had agreed to travel with me, and we rustled up formula and diapers and medications and all the special equipment that would help the sick babies get through the flight. In the midst of the frantic preparations, we got a call that I needed to get the babies' visas stamped by the local ministry of health.

"You need to appear in front of him or the babies can't leave," the message said.

We had four hours until flight time. *You've got this*, I told myself.

At the ministry, I left the babies with the nurse and was led to a room with a large number of men around a table, talking and yelling at each other in Hindi. They never addressed me—they just jabbered on and on to one another. I felt my anxiety building.

Finally, after half an hour, the minister of health turned around and looked down his nose at me in the most patronizing way possible. "You don't need to take the babies," he said. "It is a matter of national honor. We can get help for them here, in this country."

My head began whirling. The male condescension combined with the desperateness of the situation was too much to bear. Something snapped in me at that moment. I lifted my arm and then slammed my fist hard against the table.

"Goddamn it, if you can do it, then do it. Fix them right now. But you know you won't."

His eyes widened in disbelief. A woman was talking back to him! For a moment, I wondered if he would demand to have me arrested, but I didn't care. I continued in a fury.

"If you had any honor, you would have helped the babies in the beginning, but you didn't. If you had any honor, you wouldn't be disposing of little girls the way you do in this country."

Suddenly all the jabbering stopped and the room fell fully silent. The men had no intention of helping these babies, but they didn't expect I would dare call them out on it.

The minister looked at me and blinked. If he couldn't win by intimidation, he didn't want to deal with me at all. He nodded to a heavyset man sitting in the back who stamped the visas and handed me back the passports. I took them without another word and fled the room. But my heart didn't stop hammering with anxiety until we were on the plane with the wheels lifting up—and I knew we were free.

As I was heading home on that plane, I started to feel a deep bond with the baby in my arms. Phoenix Children's Hospital had agreed to handle Bridget's healthcare and then reach out to the local Bangladeshi community to find a family for her. I knew she would be well cared for and I didn't have to worry about her continuing welfare. But I realized I couldn't give this child up. Hand her to a nurse in Phoenix and not be part of her life? I couldn't do that. I had three little children at home, a large extended family, a husband in the Senate, and my own busy life of travel and political responsibilities. But I could not turn away from this small human being whose life was now in my hands.

Our commercial flight made a brief stop in Tokyo and then continued on to Los Angeles, where we transferred to a plane to Phoenix. When we finally arrived and walked down the airplane steps, a bank of cameras and reporters greeted us. I'd not had a chance to tell John my revelation about Bridget picking us as her parents, but he just seemed to know. When we exchanged those few words on the tarmac, and he agreed that Bridget would come to our house, I had every bit of confirmation that I would ever need about the kind of man he was.

A couple who lived nearby said they would care for the other baby while she was going through treatment, and they ended up having the same feeling that I did. They could never let her go. She and Bridget grew up together and have stayed close friends. Bridget has been an amazing trouper—she underwent at least a dozen surgeries over the years, all to correct various problems caused by the cleft palate. When I first brought her home, she weighed only five or six pounds, and she couldn't have the first surgery until she reached ten pounds. When I went to the grocery store with her in the baby carrier, people would peek at her and gasp. Since she couldn't easily swallow, I had to devise a way to feed her, and I came up with what was basically a giant syringe with a feeding tube on the end of it. I would slowly pump the nourishment into her and was thrilled when she started gaining weight.

Despite the surgeries and difficulties, Bridget fit into our family immediately. The boys thought of her as a toy, and as she got bigger, the only arguments were the usual ones toddlers have about who gets to play with which blocks and games. Do you want to know what really makes you feel good as a mom? When you've been teaching your children about equality and how we are all alike—and then a situation comes along where they prove just how thoroughly they have accepted that. I am proud of the spirit of acceptance my children display, but I continue to be stunned at the narrow-mindedness of so many others in our country.

The treatment of Bridget in South Carolina was my first up-close experience with racial ugliness—and I saw it all over again when our son Jack got married to Renee, a beautiful and extremely accomplished Air Force officer who is African American. The vilely intolerant comments strangers posted on Facebook and Twitter and elsewhere broke my heart.

As a major in the Air Force, Renee actually outranked Jack—but he is very protective of her and now of their biracial baby. He doesn't want them to get hurt. Jack has John's political gene, and I hope he runs for elected office someday. He has the kindness and bigger worldview that we need right now, and he also has John's ability to make everyone want to work with him. I would like to think that on whatever ballot he appears, the voters will be wise enough to be color-blind. Our world has enough divisions. We create goodness for ourselves and others when we see beyond differences and celebrate the power of compassion and hope.

PART TWO

———⬡⬡⬡———

The Politics of Courage

CHAPTER 6

—◦◦◦◦—

Out of the Bunker

Apart from the dirty tricks of South Carolina, the 2000 primary campaign held a lot of fun moments for John and me. We skipped the Iowa caucuses and focused on New Hampshire, driving through the state in the bus called the Straight Talk Express. A few reporters traveled with us full-time, and others rotated through. They enjoyed sharing ideas and discussing policy with John, and I had a good time getting to know them, too. At one point, we had two Pulitzer Prize–winning photographers riding with me in the back of the bus. I knew the photographers and reporters were there to cover the campaign, but it was also a treat just talking with them and hearing their stories. Some, like Washington correspondent Jake Tapper, have remained friends.

I loved campaigning in New Hampshire because retail politics still mattered there—and I'm sure they still do. We had to be out shaking hands and making personal connections, just like we had done in that first congressional campaign. I would get invited to have coffee with a small group of voters at someone's house, and invariably one of the people at the table would remind me that we had met a couple of weeks earlier at another coffee klatch.

Rural areas and small towns take the concept of "local" to a whole different level. After one breakfast chat, a friendly woman came up to talk to me. "It was very nice meeting you, but neither you nor Senator McCain have been to our neighborhood yet, and we'd like you to come," she said.

"We should do that," I agreed. "Where's your neighborhood?"

"About four blocks that way," she said, gesturing.

She wasn't joking. In her mind, four blocks away constituted a whole new locale of friends and neighbors.

Both major political parties talk regularly about shaking up their primary schedules to keep such a small state from having such undue influence. But the people in New Hampshire take their first-in-the-nation status seriously, and they understand that political careers can be made or broken there. (Iowa precedes New Hampshire in the primary season, but they have caucuses rather than a traditional ballot-box vote.) They respect the outsized role they play in determining the candidates for a national election and, win or lose, most candidates come to respect the New England rectitude and decency most of the voters display.

Campaigning in New Hampshire, you sit at kitchen tables and start to feel like part of the local family. I often thought how nice it would be to have our own family with us there, too. John and I didn't usually bring the children along with us during the campaign. With Meghan in high school, Jack and Jimmy in middle school, and Bridget barely nine years old, we wanted to keep their lives as unaffected as possible. Several people, including my parents, looked after them while we were away, so we didn't have to worry. But once we realized that New Hampshire voters were likely to give John an upset win over George W. Bush, we thought it would be fun to have them with us to celebrate. A young woman who spent a lot of time with our family agreed to fly with them to New Hampshire. Even from across the country, I liked to be involved in all the details of my children's lives, so I gave her lists of how to pack for them and what to bring. I forgot to mention what they should wear on the plane as they prepared to leave warm and sunny Phoenix.

The day the kids arrived, the ground was packed high with snow and the temperature hovered in the teens. Several members of the press corps were with us when we went to the airport—and so a lot of eyes watched as all four children got off the plane wearing T-shirts and flip-flops. I was completely mortified. So much for me winning Mother of the Year.

The Straight Talk Express continued on the road through March, but when it became clear that the delegate count wouldn't add up in our favor, John bowed out. He had always been a long shot, and we both felt satisfied that so many voters had liked his independent ideas. His focus on campaign finance reform drew a lot of enthusiasm from voters and the press, and in Michigan, where independents and Democrats could vote in the primary, he showed that his appeal extended well beyond the Republican core.

The South Carolina experience had been so upsetting for both of us that it took John a little while to throw his support to Bush. But he did it, meeting with his delegates before the Republican convention and telling them that their votes should go to Bush. When I heard the words, I pursed my lips hard and tried not to cry. I noticed others in the room also trying not to get emotional. They believed in John— and that meant so much. Since I was leading the Arizona delegation to the convention, I knew how much it would hurt not to get to vote for my husband. But John believed in compromise and unity, and he gave a moving speech at the convention praising Bush. He even told the story of Bush's dad, the former president, serving in the Navy under John's grandfather. To me, that was a hugely gracious gesture on John's part—giving George W. Bush some of John's hard-won military credibility.

John returned happily to the Senate, his national reputation even stronger than it had been before. He did some campaigning with Bush in the general election against Al Gore, and like everyone else in the country, we were stunned on election night when no clear winner emerged. We watched in disbelief as the results in Florida were challenged and recounts demanded. For the first time ever, I became familiar with terms like "hanging chads," the bits of paper from the hard-to-tabulate punch-card ballots that emerged from the voting machines used in some Florida counties. Eventually the whole mess ended up in the Supreme Court, which gave the election 5–4 to Bush, even though Gore had won the popular vote. Gore gave an impressive speech shortly after that, offering his concession in the name of unity and preserving democracy. He said that "partisan rancor must now be put aside." Bush then spoke about reconciliation and said he would be the president of the whole nation, not one party.

Looking back twenty years later, Bush-Gore almost seems like a proud moment in our democracy. America's strength comes from the civility of its leaders and integrity of its people. When we lose that, our nation is not the same.

A few months after Bush took office, I was at home in Phoenix with the children when the terrible events of 9/11 occurred. Nearly three thousand Americans died in the terrorist attacks on the World Trade Center and the Pentagon, and thousands of others were injured. We were among the millions of families who were deeply affected by the strike on America. The day turned our family upside down and changed so much about our children's futures.

I had risen early that morning to get the kids ready for school, and I had the television on in the kitchen when the news broke that the north tower of the World Trade Center had been hit. The first reports suggested an inexplicable accident—but when the second plane crashed into the south tower a few minutes later, it seemed clear that America was under attack. Shocked, I called every number I had for John, but I couldn't reach him. The kids started coming in for breakfast, and I tried to keep up a calm veneer for them. But I kept dashing out of the kitchen, making increasingly frantic efforts to reach John. His office sent me a copy of his schedule each week, and checking it now, I saw that he had a meeting at the Pentagon at 9:15 A.M. With the two-hour time difference to Phoenix, that meant the meeting would have started minutes earlier. I thought that coincidence was probably good. John's military instincts and global knowledge would be needed right now.

A few minutes later, that meeting took on a very different meaning when the reporter on television announced another plane attack. The Pentagon had been hit.

I tried to choke back my panic. I still hadn't reached John, and there were reports that yet another plane was heading toward the capital. The children didn't know about John's Pentagon meeting, but they were smart enough to know that their dad might be in danger. As our anxiety built, we all watched in horror as the south tower in New York collapsed.

The children responded to the shock of the morning differently. Meghan became hysterical, Jack looked stunned, and Jimmy remained quiet, sitting very still and not saying a word. Bridget was too young to know what was happening, but she grasped the concept that it was bad. The boys decided to go to school, but Meghan insisted on staying home. I kept Bridget home, too.

As I continued trying to find John, I tried not to panic. I knew the Senate had an emergency evacuation plan. I told myself that if he were on the Hill, he would be brought to a bunker for safety. Still, I kept calling and calling and calling, all through the morning.

Cell service in Washington was completely out. Finally, in the early afternoon, I got an AOL instant message from one of John's staffers in the capital. *John is here. He's safe. We are gathered at my house*. I felt a flood of relief. I had no details, but hearing anything was okay for now. When the boys came home from school that afternoon, I was able to display some modicum of sanity and tell them that their father was safe.

"Have you talked to Daddy?" Jimmy asked, as he walked in the door.

"No, he's very busy with what's going on, but he's okay," I said.

Later that evening, John finally got through with a phone call. He told me what he knew of the day's events, focusing on the bigger picture rather than his own personal experience. But I needed to know exactly what he'd been through.

"Were you at the Pentagon this morning?" I asked.

"No, the meeting had been canceled—which might have saved my life," he admitted.

He told me that all the senators had indeed been rushed into a protective bunker, but he had refused to go. Instead, he got into a car with his longtime staff member Joe Donoghue. All the streets were blocked off and they couldn't get anyplace. They finally got out and walked for miles and miles.

"The captain of the police tried to grab me, but I wouldn't go to the bunker," John said. "I told him, 'You think you're going to lock me up with these guys? You're crazy. I'm not doing it.'"

Despite all the anxiety of the day, I couldn't help smiling. Of course John McCain had refused to go into the bunker. He had crashed several airplanes and survived being a POW, and he liked to face danger instead of running from it. He approved of the other senators taking reasonable action, but he had never been the kind to retreat. In his personal code, he was forever the fighter pilot, brave and self-assured, and living outside the normal rules of safety.

As we talked, I told John how deeply affected the boys had been that morning. They were just thirteen and fifteen years old, but watching their faces as the events unfolded on television, I knew exactly where they were going and what was ahead.

"They want to be out protecting their country," I told John.

"And they probably will someday," he said.

My instinct that both Jack and Jimmy would head to the military was correct—it just didn't happen in quite the way I expected. I assumed that Jack, the oldest, would lead the way in going to the Naval Academy like his dad, grandfather, and great-grandfather before him. He did just that—but his younger brother, Jimmy, was actually the first one to see combat. When Jimmy was still in high school, he came to me and announced he wanted to join the Marines. I was stunned. The issue wasn't that he was choosing a different branch of the military—that didn't matter at all. But enlisting meant that he would go into active duty almost immediately.

I listened carefully as Jimmy told me his plan. Despite his resolve—or maybe because of it—I felt a gnawing anxiety. I needed to talk it through with John. The phone wouldn't do, so I waited until he came home that weekend.

"What are we going to do?" I asked John when we had a few minutes alone.

"Let's be rational and consider the options," John said.

"He's only seventeen. He needs a parent to sign the papers or he can't enlist. We could refuse to sign, and then he can't be a Marine."

John nodded. "Is that what you want to do?"

On one hand, it was exactly what I wanted to do. American troops had just invaded Iraq. I could keep my youngest son home and protect him from the dangers of the battlefield. Was there even another hand?

Yes, there was. I looked up at John, and he didn't have to say a word—because I immediately understood. We had raised Jimmy to believe in loyalty and honor and service. That didn't mean service when it felt convenient or safe. Like any parent with a child going into the military, I had hoped our country would be at peace while he served. But if America was asking its young people to fight a war, then the sons and daughters of senators and congressmen and presidents should serve, too.

In wanting to give service during wartime, Jimmy displayed the kind of valor that our family believed in. How would we undermine that by insisting that he not enlist right now? We could give him reasons—pointing out, for example, that since he was only seventeen, he might want to have more years of school behind him before making this decision. But then he would see that the values we cared about so dearly were only theoretical, and our beliefs in sacrifice and contributing to the greater good stopped at our own front door.

"I guess if he wants to be a Marine, we should support the decision," I told John. "I'll go to the enlistment center."

"Will you be okay?" John asked.

I nodded. If I could be as grown-up and brave as my baby son, I would be okay. What greater gift can we give our children than to let them set their own course and follow their own ambitions.

The certainty I felt about supporting Jimmy's decision when I sat calmly discussing it with John disappeared on the sunny afternoon when I actually walked into the recruitment office to sign his papers. A couple of people who recognized me stood at attention when I entered—which just made it harder. *I can't believe I'm doing this*, I thought. A Marine recruiter handed me the paperwork, and I studied it for a long time. I could try to frame it however I wanted, but in the end a single truth haunted me. By signing, I was sending my underage son into combat. For the hundredth time that day, I ran through the conversation I'd had about this with Jimmy.

"You know what you're doing, right?" I'd asked him.

"Yes. Completely," he said.

"No second thoughts?"

"None."

I put pen to paper and quickly signed.

Jimmy graduated high school and left shortly afterward for boot camp in San Diego. As boot camp graduation approached, John and I agreed that our whole family would go to celebrate Jimmy's achievement and show our support. The ceremony is a big deal for families and filled with mixed emotions: the pride that your child is now a Marine commingling with the anxious knowledge that he will soon go into combat. I held John's hand as the newly minted graduates marched forward in neat rows. The moment I caught sight of Jimmy, I burst into tears. I was overwhelmed to see how much he had matured in just thirteen weeks. Our squirrelly teenage son had become a young man with confidence and self-esteem. He stood straight and tall like all Marines do, and he looked so adult. I also knew what was next for him.

We held a dinner for Jimmy that night in San Diego with family and friends. John's presence at the graduation had attracted a lot of attention. The Iraq War was hot and heavy by then, and John had been extremely vocal about it. Jimmy admitted that he had come in for some extra razzing and hazing because his dad was so well known. Instructors at boot camp were particularly rough on him, trying to see if they could make the senator's son drop out. Jack later coped with a similar situation in the Naval Academy. Having some degree of fame serves as a kind of inverse privilege in the military. The better known you are, the tougher everyone makes it for you. The boys endured a lot for being McCains.

After San Diego, Jimmy went to Camp Pendleton, just up the coast, for his infantry training. A few months later, he got notice that he was being deployed to Anbar Province, an al-Qaeda stronghold in the west of Iraq that the Marines had been trying to control. Sharing a border with Syria, it was an important area for both sides with incredibly complicated politics—an insurgency movement and then a counterinsurgency meant there was rampant and continuing violence. The Marines hoped that securing the area might be a step toward peacefully rebuilding Iraq. But every story I read about Ramadi, the capital, involved sniper fire, chemical weapons, and suicide attacks.

I went to see Jimmy off at the first leg of his journey—a bus that would take him to March Air Reserve Base to fly out. John decided not to join me. He worried that his being there would make the moment about him rather than Jimmy. I knew he was right, but I felt irrationally angry at being left alone for this painful and poignant ordeal. Jimmy got on the bus, carrying a weapon across his body that seemed bigger than he was. He waved goodbye, and then the door closed.

I thought I would be okay, but just then a little five-year-old boy ran up to the bus and started banging on the door. "Daddy, don't go, Daddy, don't go!" he cried. As tears streamed down his face, I lost my composure, too. Would his daddy ever come back? Would my Jimmy? Every single person standing by that bus shared his torment.

When your children go off to college or to their first job, you miss them, but you can rely on staying connected with calls or texts or pictures on social media. Not so when your child goes off to the military. The Marines in Anbar Province didn't have email or regular access to phones. They did have a one-way messaging system called MotoMail. I could type a message on the computer, send it to the address for Jimmy's company, and in twenty-four hours or so, they would print it out and deliver it to him. Jimmy couldn't reply, but I still sent a lot of MotoMails. His company also had a satellite phone, and sometimes he could call from that.

I knew that Jimmy was stationed in an area of heavy combat. One night he called me when he was on guard duty and all seemed quiet.

Standing high up on a watchtower, he described his view looking out at the stars, and he spoke so beautifully that I could practically see the stars twinkling, too. Given the late hour, nobody else wanted the satellite phone, so we chatted comfortably, and I almost convinced myself not to worry.

Suddenly, though, in the midst of my relating some family story, I heard Jimmy shout, "Oh, no! Incoming!" And the phone went dead. (His words were a little more graphic than "Oh, no.")

I held on to the phone for a minute, hoping it might ring again and Jimmy would come back to say that all was okay. But I realized that his night had gone in a very different direction than expected.

Desperate for information, I turned on the television to an all-news station. I knew it was unlikely that they would have any reports this quickly, and probably not at all, but I watched for a while to have some distraction.

John had a policy of not talking to me about where Jimmy was, or what was happening in Anbar Province. I understood that he was privy to confidential information about the war—but this was our son, for heaven's sake. I needed to know. My only source of information was Lindsey Graham, the Republican senator from South Carolina who was close to John and a dear family friend. He always tried to help me, whatever it took, and we had a bond that went well beyond politics. I made myself wait until the next morning when information could have filtered back to the United States—and then I called Lindsey.

I told him what had happened on my call with Jimmy. "I'm sure he's okay," I said, "but do you mind finding out?"

A few hours later, Lindsey reported that fighting in the area was fierce, but Jimmy was okay. I felt a lot of relief and a little bit of guilt, too. Other military families didn't have my access to information, and I knew how painful it was to be left in limbo, uncertain of the fate of someone you loved. Most of the time, I shared that sense of anxiety and dread. My greatest support came from a group called Blue Star Mothers, which I discovered late one night when I couldn't sleep and began cruising the Internet. The organization of moms supports our troops in combat—and supports one another. I turned to them regularly. Someone always seemed to know which rumors were true and which were false, and we could share both our pride and our trepidation. The Blue Star moms have a special service flag, and I have kept one on my door for many years. We are a three-star family, since my two sons and daughter-in-law are all in the active military.

Jimmy remained in the Marines for five years and two deployments, and he saw some truly horrific things. Some of the stories he told when he returned shocked me. But like John, he could also spin a story for its humor and humanity. During the 2008 presidential campaign, Jimmy came home shortly before the convention that would nominate his dad. A big group was gathered at our cabin in northern Arizona, and one evening turned into a big party, with seven or eight U.S. senators, three or four governors, several members of Congress, and various people involved in the campaign.

At one point, I looked over and saw Jimmy holding court with some of the most powerful people in the country—all of them hanging on his every word. None of his listeners had been in the military, but they listened spellbound as Jimmy told a few frightening stories and some hysterically funny ones, too. Long into the night, the room filled with raucous laughter as Jimmy shared his experiences with wit and insight. Watching him, I admired how confident he had become, how at ease he seemed in the world. I'd often heard John talk about how being in the military gave you a new maturity, but now I could see it close up. I sent off a boy and got back a man.

. . .

John supported the Bush administration's 2003 decision to go to war with Iraq and topple Saddam Hussein, and he advocated for the U.S. troop surge to secure more of the region a couple of years later. His confidence in the rightness of the cause might have contributed to Jimmy's desire to enlist. I never questioned John's views, but I also admired that he could take in new information and change his stance. Many years later, John came around to the position that the Iraq War had been a mistake. Many of the claims that the Bush administration had made to support the war never held up, and the main rationale for the war—that Iraq possessed weapons of mass destruction— turned out to be simply false. While some people continued to see the Iraq War as retaliation for 9/11, the al-Qaeda terrorists had no links to Iraq.

"America was wrong to invade Iraq," John told me at one point, "and I have to take some share of the blame."

"You weren't the commander in chief," I reminded him.

"I believed the information and thought we could win," he said. "People might have paid attention if I took the other side."

Many elected officials were duped by incorrect information in the buildup to that war and never made apologies. But John lived by his own code of honor—and he would never let past errors slide by. Toward the end of his life, he publicly declared the war a mistake and apologized for any part he'd played. He mourned the hundreds of thousands of lives lost on both sides. I think military officers like John who served during Vietnam never quite got over that defeat. Perhaps they hoped that with Iraq, they could restore American pride and show how wars could be fought and won. It was one of the many dreams that didn't survive America's incursions in the Middle East.

CHAPTER 7

Rekindling Hope

The challenge of being married to a famous person may not sound like a problem worthy of much sympathy, but I think many women face similar hurdles in trying to find a balance in their lives. It's gratifying to be one-half of a partnership and have your life fully intertwined with the person you love. But there's a yearning to be an independent person in your own right, too. As John rocketed to the top of his profession and became a familiar figure around the world, I had to figure out who I was. In most political marriages, one person gets all the attention while the other boosts and supports and encourages. Sometimes when John was traveling and constantly in the news, I wished he could concentrate more on us. But I never resented my role, and I decided that instead of yearning for a more balanced partnership, I would simply try appreciating all the amazing experiences that opened up for me.

Because John and I had different locations, the two distinctive sides of my life were clear. At home in Phoenix, I was a mom completely involved with my children and family and volunteer organizations. When I went to Washington, I entered John's orbit and gave myself over to extraordinary experiences like meeting presidents and world leaders and having dinner at the White House—an incredibly special experience each time we did it.

From the first days of our marriage, John and I traveled together extensively. He stayed open to everything when he visited a new location, and he reveled in meeting new people and discovering different views. Nowadays, I am comfortable going anywhere in the world on my own, and I got much of that sense of ease from watching John. Since John was opposed to boondoggles of all kinds, I didn't join him very often on his Senate trips. When I did, I made sure to pay for myself. But over the years, we often traveled as a family, and some of my favorite trips were just the two of us.

Early in our marriage we took a trip to South Africa that was notably eye-opening for me. The country is now a popular location for Americans and Europeans going on luxury safaris and taking in the natural beauty, but at that time, apartheid was still in place and the world was divided on how to respond. John arranged for us to meet a few of the country's leaders, including one who represented the Afrikaners, the National Party, which opposed integration and wanted to continue white minority rule.

I felt conflicted during those meetings. It's important to listen to many viewpoints, but to me, that doesn't mean all are equally valid. However they justified it, the Afrikaners' position had allowed the powerful white elite to maintain their status by stomping on the country's vast majority of black people. I had been raised in privileged circumstances, but my dad grew up poor. He rose in life because he lived in the United States at a time when social mobility was still possible. I couldn't imagine anything more horrifying than deciding a person's fate at birth and then making the obstacles to any change insurmountable.

The Afrikaner we met with was big, burly, and intimidating. He was ardent in his position and heated in his presentation. His views were antithetical to ours on every ground. John tried to present the anti-apartheid stance, but the NP guy remained vehement. I realized then how difficult it is to shake people from beliefs they have held their whole life.

After that disquieting discussion, I was thrilled when our next meeting brought us face-to-face with Desmond Tutu, the religious leader and human rights activist who stood up against apartheid. I sat in the meeting with him and John and listened in complete awe. Reverend Tutu must have felt the same anger as every other black person in South Africa, but he tempered his comments with humor and warmth. His words rang with insight. Instead of being intimidated, I was simply mesmerized by his wisdom and inclusive views. A year or so later, in 1984, Tutu won the Nobel Peace Prize. He became an important leader in the negotiations that finally ended fifty years of apartheid in 1993 and ushered in the government of Nelson Mandela.

Experiences you have when you are in your twenties and still impressionable can have lifelong impact. I admired Tutu when I met him, and his advocacy for equal rights for gays and lesbians, blacks, and women became ingrained in my own belief system. By the time he visited America in 1984, he was widely beloved, often drawing comparisons to Martin Luther King, Jr. He met with Ronald Reagan on that trip. Though Tutu objected to the president's position on South Africa and charged that his actions hurt blacks in both countries, they remained cordial and had a frank and open discussion.

In my own human rights work now, I think often of that encounter with Tutu in his home country. I understand that trying to make positive change in the world can be tiring and frustrating, and it's always easier to stay back quietly than go out and resist the wrongs that have become part of the fabric of your society. But the tireless efforts of people like Desmond Tutu, Nelson Mandela, and Martin Luther King, Jr., eventually helped penetrate some of the inequities.

With those great leaders, John shared a similar openness of spirit and desire to move on from past conflicts—an attitude that is both profoundly important and extraordinarily hard to attain. One year, John planned an amazing trip to Vietnam for our family, including visits to the mountainous northern region of the country populated by the Hmong people, and other spots that tourists don't usually go. It always amazed me that John could embrace the new Vietnam. He was fascinated by what the country had become, and held no bitterness for his years as a POW. The children knew that their dad had been tortured and imprisoned on this land, but they also saw that he was able to look beyond himself and his own experiences. That he could have such an expansive view made a profound impression on me, too. Without his saying a word, I was moved by the extraordinarily hopeful message that with the right resolve, we can all make the future better than the past.

I always took good care of my health. I ate a balanced diet with healthy foods, walked or exercised regularly, and maintained a normal weight. I had also picked up John's attitude of feeling slightly invulnerable and confident that I could handle anything on my own. When my internist told me I had chronic high blood pressure and should start some medication, I decided to try a different approach. Pills had certainly done me no good in the past—and while I didn't worry about getting addicted to blood pressure meds, they seemed unnecessary. I decided I would handle the problem with lifestyle. I made sure to eat plenty of fruits and vegetables, which I like anyway, and kept my salt intake very low. I'm a morning person and I didn't always get enough rest, so now I made a point of going to sleep a little bit earlier. People told me that I looked good, and I equated that with being healthy. Like John, I could do it my way.

One day in 2004, I went out to lunch in Phoenix with some

friends, and we were chatting happily when I started to feel strange. I sat up a little straighter and continued the conversation. But as one of my friends told me later, "One moment you were talking normally, and the next the words were completely garbled, and nothing made sense."

I remember hearing someone ask, "Cindy, are you okay?" as I slumped back in my seat. I had a sense of everyone anxiously rushing around me. I wanted to tell them that all would be fine and they shouldn't worry, but I couldn't formulate the words. My friends suspected that I was having a stroke, and they wisely rushed me to Barrow Neurological Institute, a medical center in Phoenix with a world-class reputation.

Strokes come in many varieties. The most common is a ministroke, officially called a TIA, or transient ischemic attack. The patient has all the signs of a stroke because a part of the brain doesn't get enough blood flow for a time. But it goes away in twenty-four hours or so and doesn't leave any permanent effects. Mine was different.

"You had a serious stroke," the doctor told me, when I finally recovered enough to register what someone was saying. I couldn't form any words in response, but the thought in my head was *"Serious" sounds like the understatement of the year.*

I had suffered a full bleed—which means that blood vessels in my head had popped and bled into the brain. You can die easily from that. A drug called tPA (tissue plasminogen activator) administered within three hours can stop or reverse some symptoms and make recovery more likely. I got the tPA in time, and it probably saved my life.

A stroke occurs suddenly, with absolutely no warning. One minute I was fine and the next I was on the floor, unable to speak. Meghan was off in college, but Jack, Jimmy, and Bridget were still at home. They had their usual day of school and after-school sports and came home surprised to find they were alone. Nobody knew why I wasn't there until one of them turned on the television and heard a news report that Cindy McCain had been hospitalized with a stroke. It's awful to think that my children learned what happened to me from TV. We never found out who at the hospital leaked the news, but I hope they understand how despicable it was. Sharing private information isn't a game—we're talking about real people's lives and children's well-being.

John was also caught completely off guard. Given the time difference, he was at a dinner in New York City, seated next to then-mayor Michael Bloomberg, when someone finally got word through to him. He started to make arrangements to get back to Phoenix, but Mayor Bloomberg cut that off quickly. "Just get up and leave," he said. "I'll call my plane for you." When I heard about that later, I felt the deepest gratitude for his incredible kindness. Our families became friends after that, and he and John developed a close relationship. Like all of us, Bloomberg has made some mistakes in his political life, but he is sincerely philanthropic and a person you can count on in a crisis. He did many great things to improve New York City, and for John and me, he made one awful day in our lives slightly easier.

I spent three weeks in the hospital, and my memories from the time are blurry. I had a vague sense of the children coming to visit and John being at my bedside and holding my hand. When I finally came home, I walked with a limp, one of my arms wouldn't work, and a side of my face drooped. Even more frightening, when I tried to talk, I couldn't find the words. The sounds came out slurred and unintelligible. So I went back to Barrow for outpatient rehabilitation. It was hard work and the improvements sometimes seemed torturously slow, but I reminded myself that I didn't have it nearly as bad as some other people. I saw many patients whose strokes had left them far more debilitated than I was, and I knew that I had a chance to fight my way back to health. I was only fifty years old, and I wasn't giving up yet.

In my mind, I couldn't remain weak because I had too much to do. I had to get up and going. John was a constant inspiration to me. I knew he had come home from his imprisonment with a leg that was completely stiff and damaged arms and shoulder—and look what he had done. Who was I not to be able to overcome my setback?

John had always been stoic about his injuries, but he didn't expect that of me. He was kind and encouraging, and understood when I shed some tears. One night when we shared stories about painful physical therapy, we ended up laughing rather than crying.

"I didn't expect this misery to be a bonding experience," I told him. "Thank you for staying so positive."

"You're going to get through this," he said. "When you're in the midst, it feels like it will never end. But you keep going and moving forward—and suddenly you're looking back on the pain rather than living it."

I knew he was speaking from experience, so his perspective gave me the boost I needed. Through the days and weeks of rehab, my physical symptoms started to recede and my speech improved. After a couple of months, I expressed my gratitude to the team at Barrow and decided that the rest was up to me. Summer was approaching, and instead of staying in Phoenix, I wanted to be by myself and focus fully on getting well. With the kids in high school and college and busy with activities of their own, they could handle a few months without me. If I wanted to be any kind of wife and mother moving forward, I had to put myself back together.

I planned to rent a place in Coronado, California, a pretty town in the San Diego Bay. I love the ocean. In Coronado, I could walk every day along the beach and be totally within my own head, rather than worrying what someone else needed. Phoenix was close enough that John and kids could come visit me.

"I don't like the idea of your being there alone," John said when I first proposed the plan.

"I need to take care of myself and get well. It won't help to have people around feeling bad for me."

"I'm glad you want to push forward, but you've been through a lot."

"That's life," I reminded him. "You've been through a lot. Bridget's been through a lot. When it's time to break out a pity party for me, I'll let you know."

John gave a little smile. He usually liked to take charge of a situation, but on the occasions when I let my steel backbone show, he appreciated that, too. He had grown up with strong McCain women, and while his instinct was to take care of his wife, he admired grit and mettle. He also knew that arguing wouldn't do any good—I had already signed the rental agreement.

Those few months in Coronado were the best gift I could have given myself. I had no responsibilities beyond getting well. I followed the diet I had been given: virtually no sodium and very low sugar. I walked and walked and walked, trying to get my strength back up. The stroke had left me with a bit of a limp, but by the end of the summer, I was striding almost normally. My arm had been weakened, and that, too, improved. Many days, after I finished walking, I sat looking out at the ocean and spinning big thoughts about the meaning of existence and what I still wanted to achieve. I didn't know if John would want to run for the presidency again, but I had to get myself in order for whatever we decided to do together.

I pondered my personal goals, too. My life could have ended that day at the restaurant, but I'd been given more time to be with my children and continue building a legacy. In some ways, we are only what we leave behind. Before the stroke, I had already dedicated myself to some philanthropic organizations, including CARE, which helps fight children's poverty and hunger, and Operation Smile, providing life-changing surgeries to children around the world born with cleft palates. I was involved with HALO, the nonprofit that removes the scourge of land mines left over from war, which Princess Diana made famous—and my work with all of them felt good and important. During those days in Coronado, I determined that I would double down on the causes I cared about, and try to provide the sense of hope and possibility in others that I was now rekindling in myself. We have only so much time. We need to use it well.

I came back to Phoenix at the end of the summer in good shape and feeling emotionally stronger, too. Only a few problems lingered. I had lost a lot of weight from the stroke and gotten way too thin, and the summer hadn't helped that problem. But I knew I could slowly start gaining a few pounds back. On top of that, I still had short-term memory loss—and while that has since improved dramatically, it continues to plague me from time to time. I can remember things from the long-ago past, but more immediate experiences don't always register well. Ask me who I met yesterday, and I can probably visualize the people in the room but maybe not recall their names. (I hope they don't think I'm rude if we meet again.) The shaky memory is one aftereffect I haven't been able to fully overcome.

You find ways to work around challenges. I keep a really accurate calendar and a diary of daily events so I won't get an event or a date wrong. I used to tell myself that I had to be extra vigilant because I didn't want to embarrass John—but he never got upset about things like that. It is more about my own self-esteem.

I've learned more about strokes than I ever wanted to know, and I am far more aware of signs and symptoms now. I take my own blood pressure regularly so I can monitor what's going on. Once you've had a stroke, there's a higher likelihood of suffering another, so I walk a lot and take my meds. Both of my parents had high blood pressure and I have been told over and over again that mine is hereditary and not stress-related. In some ways, I think that's an advantage. Given all the political drama in my life, if it were stress-related, I'd probably be dead by now.

Everyone goes through hard times of one sort or another, and John had showed that what really makes a difference is the perspective you bring. Whether dealing with his years as a POW, his physical disabilities, or his loss in 2000, his attitude was always to remain positive and look for the good. Find the next good experience you can move on to. In that spirit, I continued with one of the craziest adventures of my life not long after the stroke—a sport called drift racing.

I've always loved car racing. During the 2008 campaign, the staff knew that whenever I appeared bogged down or tired, they could send me to a NASCAR race and I would immediately cheer up. I loved the crowds and the camaraderie and the energy. I got to attend races at Daytona and Darlington and Nashville during the campaign, and I cheered and roared at all of them. At one event, the organizer agreed to let me drive the pace car.

"Take it slow and do one lap," he said nervously.

I nodded, but getting behind the wheel was so much fun that I zoomed around for an extra lap.

It's not just NASCAR that appeals to me. When I was young, my dad had been part owner of an Indy car driven by the great racer Bobby Unser, and I used to attend the Indy 500 with my dad before they allowed women in the pits. That sexist rule finally changed when I was in high school—and attending that year was a great highlight for me. Women were in the pits and the world did not fall apart!

If you want to hang out with your children, it helps to share their interests. So when Jack got excited about drift racing during high school, I happily started learning about it. I'd never seen a drift race before. It turned out to be a crazy form of racing where you basically skid around the track, barely keeping the car under control. The nose of the car is below the backside, and the imbalance makes the car slide sideways when you're going fast or turning.

Jack saw a couple of races, and then he asked if I wanted to build a car and race with him. I looked at him in surprise. Some races have one driver and some have two people in the car. Jack planned on competing in the two-person events.

"You want your mom as a teammate?" I asked.

"Why not?" he said. "You're cool."

When your teenage son calls you cool, you're immediately willing to do anything for him. If Jack and I were going to race, we needed our own car—and we started building one together. Jack picked the body and the frame and then we began tweaking it, putting on heavyweight roll bars and other equipment needed to make it legal for racing and also as secure and safe as it could be. For his spring break, he asked if we could go to Japan, where the sport started. I agreed to take Jack and Jimmy and a group of their friends—and the squad of boys decided they wanted to make the trip all about cars.

"That's fine, and there's only one thing I'm going to ask for," I said. "I want to go to the Mikimoto pearl farm in northern Japan."

"Okay, Mom, we can do that," Jack said.

We spent a week in Japan and had a great time focused on cars—building them, racing them, manufacturing them. We visited tracks that were meccas for drift racers, and Jack got a chance to meet some of the Japanese racers who were very well known—for him, it was the equivalent of going one-on-one with LeBron James. Our day trip to Mikimoto Pearl Island also turned out to be interesting for the boys. They helped me pick out pearls for a necklace, and the jewelers on-site created an exquisite four-strand pearl necklace for me. We all marveled at how perfect it was, and when I put it on, the boys grinned.

"You look like a queen, Mom," Jack said.

Maybe not a queen—but I did feel pretty special. I have continued to wear and love the necklace. It's extra-special for me because it
comes with such warm memories of traveling in Japan and having the
boys at my side.

We returned from that trip two days before my stroke, so the car-
racing excitement got put on hold for a while. But many months later
when I was back from rehab and Coronado and beginning to feel like
myself again, Jack surprised me with a present of professional driving
lessons. I hesitated, worried that I might still be too weak to take on
something so strenuous. I didn't even know if my hand had recovered
well enough to grip a stick shift.

"Come on, Mom, you can do this," Jack said.

"I'm not sure," I admitted.

"It will be fun. Besides, we're going to do this three-day course
together."

How could I say no to that? With Jack at my side, I took the driving lessons and felt a certain thrill in realizing what I could do on a
track. Part of the course was escape and evasion, so I learned how to
take a curve at high speed and get out of a spin. It did a lot for my
self-esteem and helped me get my confidence back. Afterward, Jack
asked if I wanted to do one more drift race with him before he headed
back to the Naval Academy. Still shaky but eager, I agreed, and we
went to compete at a small race in Phoenix. The adrenaline began
flowing in both of us as soon as we got onto the track.

"Whoo-hoo, this is great!" I said exuberantly as Jack rounded the
first turn.

We went just a little farther—and the bumper fell off the car.

"I've got it!" I told Jack.

He pulled over and stopped the car. I grabbed the bumper from
the track and threw it in the back. I got back into my seat and we
continued the race. When we crossed the finish line, my skin felt
sweaty and hot, and I was breathing hard from the excitement and

the physical strains of competing. But as I climbed out of the car, I felt a complete thrill at what we'd done. Every nerve in my body felt charged and alive. Later, it occurred to me that after a medical setback, your first goal is simply to survive. But then your aim should be truly to *live*—fully and vibrantly. If drift racing helped me do that, maybe I could be ready for races of a different kind.

CHAPTER 8

———∞———

Running for President

Maybe because travel was such a big part of our lives, John popped the big question to me on a romantic trip. No, he didn't ask me to marry him—that had happened years earlier. On this trip, he asked me to run with him for president for a second time.

John suggested the two of us take a trip to the Maldives, a chain of exquisite small islands in the Indian Ocean. We rented a boat and spent the first day catching fish. As evening fell, we attached the boat to an offshore anchor, waded in, and barbecued on the beach. In the idyllic setting, with a crew to take care of the sailing, both of us relaxed. The boat itself was small and rugged—no luxury cruiser—but that was just the way we liked it.

John waited until the last night to make his tender proposal. We'd been talking and laughing all day and had that rekindling of romance that happens with long-married couples on picturesque vacations. I had an exotic island drink in my hand and the wind was ruffling my hair. John leaned over and took my free hand in both of his.

"Cindy, I'd like to formally ask you to run for president with me," he said.

As with most proposals, you know it might happen at some point, but you're still caught off guard.

I looked out at the setting sun sparkling on the waves and took another sip of my drink.

"I don't know what to say," I admitted.

"Say 'yes,'" John said. "I want you at my side and I won't go ahead without you."

By then, it was 2006. The world had changed since John's last run. The terrorist attacks of 9/11 had transformed American foreign policy. Jimmy was serving in Iraq, and Jack was in the Naval Academy. John never talked about the boys or used their service for political gain, but during a presidential run, the media would shine a spotlight that could potentially put them further into harm's way. And what about Bridget? What additional personal assaults would she have to face? I had learned in 2000 that even the most innocent and vulnerable family members are never off-limits to scheming political operatives. As a mom, I wanted to protect my family and keep them safe. As a wife, I wanted to help my husband achieve all he could and reach the pinnacle he deserved.

I tried to evaluate all the other potential issues, too. My own humanitarian work would have to take a backseat for the duration of the campaign, but I knew that I would pick it up again when I could. My stroke didn't have much effect on how I thought about another presidential bid. I was mostly healthy again. My short-term memory remained disrupted, and sometimes I had a little weakness in my hand, but it was nothing consequential enough to hold me back. Emotionally, I had been recharged and had a sense of making the most of every day. Part of me believed that meant seeking adventure and new experiences.

The run in 2000 had been relatively short, and we'd started it with few expectations on us. But I expected that if John ran again, it would be more of a grind. Instead of a long shot, he would be a real contender, and the press would surely become harsher. Usually when John brought up the possibility of another run, I didn't say much, but he heard my unstated preference. *No, don't run. We're happy now. Let's safeguard our happy family.*

But sitting in the peaceful Maldives, all seemed possible. I knew that John wasn't making his proposal lightly. His campaign team must have told him now was the time, and I expected that they had all signed on for the race. If I said no, and I really meant it, John would pull the plug on the whole process. I couldn't do that. I had voiced my objections, and he knew the reality as well as I did. Here was the chance of a lifetime for someone truly qualified to bring change to our country. Who was I to stop him?

"This has been such a fun trip," I said to John. "Really the best. I loved everything about it."

John looked at me, trying to figure out how that answered his proposal.

"If you run, can we promise to still have fun?"

Now he smiled and a wave of relief seemed to pass over his face.

"It won't be fun every minute," he admitted. "But we'll do our best."

"Proposal accepted," I said.

He didn't have a diamond ring handy, so we sealed the deal with a kiss.

When you look back on an election, the conclusion seems almost inevitable. This is what happened, so this is what had to happen. You can recognize trends and story lines that led to the ultimate result. But in the midst of the campaign, every decision has a consequence, and small decisions can lead to outcomes with profound national and international ramifications.

I often wondered what would have happened if John had won the

nomination in 2000, and then the presidency. Perhaps his understanding of global intelligence could have created a different situation around 9/11. Maybe John would have paid more attention to the
early warnings about al-Qaeda and taken preemptive action. We can
never know—but as our family geared up for the run in 2008, it made
me all the more determined that we do everything right. I believed in
John and was convinced he could make America better and stronger.

With George W. Bush finishing his second term as president, the
Republican field for president in 2008 was wide open. Vice President
Dick Cheney decided not to run, and so did Secretary of State Con-
doleezza Rice—but others flooded into the race. Early polls tried to
figure out which contender was most likely to beat Hillary Clinton,
since at that point, everyone assumed she would be the Democratic
nominee. The actual nominee, of course, turned out to be Barack
Obama.

Pundits and pollsters are wrong often enough to prove William
Goldman's famous observation "Nobody knows anything." The
Oscar-winning screenwriter directed his comment toward Hollywood, where he insisted not one person in the motion picture business could judge ahead of time whether a movie was going to work.
But he might as well have been discussing political campaigns. You
can't predict smash hits in movies and you can't predict winners in
politics. Who would have guessed that a barely known African American senator named Barack Hussein Obama would become a two-
term president? But in this campaign, I started to learn that history
doesn't just happen to us. The decisions we make every day, big and
small, can change our futures.

Campaigns for president begin ridiculously early. By late 2006,
with the election still more than two years away, John and every other
potential candidate had to begin raising money for the long, expensive run ahead. The Pulitzer Prize–winning journalist David Broder,
a long-admired member of the Washington press corps, once wryly

remarked that anybody who wants to be president so badly that he'll spend two years organizing and campaigning for it probably shouldn't be trusted with the office. John would have agreed, but there's not much you can do to buck the system. All the meetings about strategy and plans and fundraising left him cranky and frustrated. He wanted to be out talking to people and sharing his ideas, not stuck at his desk figuring out the right wording for donor requests. Much as John left the details of family events to me, he left the details of his campaign to a few staffers—and that proved to be an early disaster. They hired too many people, spent too much money, and turned our formerly cozy Straight Talk Express bus into a rolling Ritz. I didn't need that, and the bloated expenditures drove John crazy.

For a while, John seemed to be the Republican Party's great hope, and the press declared him the front-runner. But a few months in, we started noticing some strange goings-on with the campaign finances which soon bottomed out from mismanagement and overspending. John's campaign staff underwent a big shake-up.

A campaign that's on a steady course isn't much fun for the press to cover. But if it's soaring or sinking, there's a juicy angle. The campaign's financial problems changed the narrative, and suddenly all anyone wanted to discuss was how John seemed to be losing momentum. A reporter for *The New Yorker* said the campaign "seemed to spontaneously combust in a puff of fund-raising troubles and staff intrigue." In addition to whatever funny business had occurred with the finances, John wasn't getting the big donations his team had expected—especially in comparison with the Democratic candidates. Both Hillary Clinton and Barack Obama were amassing large war chests. By July 2007, there were stories everywhere that John McCain, the Republican front-runner, had fallen back in the primary pack. At this point, not a single primary had yet been held and not a single vote had been cast! I stuck to my usual position of supporting John and trying to keep him calm.

John never talked about dropping out, and if he had brought it up, I would have disagreed. He was pursuing his dream, and attacks from the press weren't going to throw him off. The press attacks were a bit of an ego blow, but I knew in my heart that he'd pull it out.

John supported the war in Iraq, and he was willing to campaign on the issue. While most Americans were disheartened and wanted to get out, John thought that a rapid departure would cause further upheaval in the region. He knew by then that we had gotten into the war on faulty intelligence, but now that we were there, he supported a surge—sending in more troops under General David Petraeus to fight the insurgency and give the Iraqis a chance to reclaim their country.

John knew his position wouldn't go over well in New Hampshire, where he needed to win the primary to have any chance in the race. Some advisers in his campaign urged him to temper his stance, but that wasn't John—he wouldn't change his views on military strategy for a campaign. He was always willing to get new information, though, and see how situations looked on the ground. Along with two of his Senate friends, John went off to Iraq in early July, and he called me one day to say how incredibly heartened he had been to witness a reenlistment ceremony. Hundreds of American soldiers, many of them immigrants, had signed on for another round of duty. Seeing their commitment reminded him what it meant to have genuine loyalty to your country—in many cases, to a country where they weren't even yet citizens.

John came home from that trip determined to stand by his position on the surge. We joked that he was possibly the only person who returned from a trip to a war-torn country feeling strong and empowered. He decided that when he visited New Hampshire now, he would stick by his positions, talk honestly about the war and the surge, and see where it led.

With his campaign funds down and staff cut, John returned to the style of campaigning that he actually liked. He did small events at veterans' halls and American Legion posts and talked with local groups. Instead of having a big entourage, he carried his own bags. A widely circulated picture of John bringing his own suitcase onto a Southwest flight probably did as much as anything to reset the trajectory of the campaign—from heading down to heading back up. He looked humble, like a guy who was campaigning for all the right reasons. It made me happy to see, because I knew the humility was real.

As things started turning around again for John, I had a brief health setback. I'd suffered from a bum knee ever since I fell off a balance beam in high school. In my early forties, I'd had a full knee replacement surgery. Nobody told me that given the technology of artificial knees at the time and my relatively young age, the replacement knee wouldn't last forever. So I was taken by surprise when the artificial knee wore out, and simple activities like walking or going up stairs left me miserable and in intense pain. I wanted to be available for John, but when the doctors said I needed a second knee replacement immediately, I didn't have much choice. Wincing in pain as I stood by John wasn't going to be helpful for either of us.

I had the surgery in October and took six weeks or so to recover. Then I joined John again on the trail. Before long, I was back to twelve-hour days of speeches, travel, and public events. I usually landed in a hotel room at night too tired to do much more than take off my shoes and makeup and fall into bed. Despite the rigors of campaigning, I tried to be a little careful about my health. I didn't want to have another stroke, so now I took the blood pressure medication that the doctor prescribed. I realized what a mistake it had been to skip that precaution before. I tried eating well and exercising like I always did, but it's difficult to maintain a clean diet when you're constantly on the road. You find a lot more cookies than fruit on a campaign bus, and local events generally run more to french fries and donuts than to fine dining. I just had to do the best I could.

I still got the migraine headaches that had tortured me for so many years, and I wasn't going to let myself be hospitalized or take opioids again to lessen their intensity. Sometimes when confronted with very bright stage or TV lights, I wore sunglasses to prevent a sudden onset. The press took the sunglasses as a sign of my being distant or arrogant, and portrayed me in ways I couldn't even recognize. No, I wasn't looking to emulate Anna Wintour, the glamorous editor of *Vogue* who was known at the time for never taking off her sunglasses. I just wanted to hold off one of the serious headaches that sometimes landed me in a hospital. In a campaign, labels like this adhere to you, whether they're true or not. Those who read about me during the 2008 campaign heard that I was cold and aloof. I never tried to refute it, because what could I say? *No, really, I'm a lot of fun! People like me!* Then you're not just cold and aloof—you've also written the *Saturday Night Live* sketch about yourself.

Maybe I should have confessed to the migraines, but it sounded to me like whining. It was my nature not to complain—and watching John stay stoic and strong over the years had made me even more intent on resisting any weakness. At one campaign stop, an avid McCain fan shook my hand so vigorously that I ended up in the hospital with a sprained wrist. Hearing about that, one reporter referred to me as "delicate." That label stung, too. Whatever health issues I've had, I don't think of myself as delicate. But I couldn't let someone else change the person I wanted to be.

The early primaries are a struggle for momentum. Iowa, a state of three million people, has disproportionate power because it holds the first-in-the-nation caucus during each presidential primary season.

The press descends on the state and gives its voters outsized importance. John opposed corn-ethanol subsidies, which he knew would be a problem for voters in Iowa. Since he wouldn't change his position—of course—he didn't commit much time or resources there.

We had loved campaigning in New Hampshire in 2000, and John was happy to focus a lot of energy there again. Mitt Romney, the governor of Massachusetts, was from the neighboring state, so we knew he had an advantage. But John did his favorite type of retail campaigning—going to local events, meeting people, sitting at a diner and sharing ideas. Though my knee surgery meant I would join him later than I'd hoped, I had fond memories from New Hampshire and was excited to be there with John again.

The first day I got there, the press made a big deal of my arrival, and we did a town hall event at a local fire station. John was already in place when I got there, and when I stepped inside, people rose and cheered. I was humbled to be welcomed back in such a warm way to the state that had given John a big victory a few years earlier. Being at a neighborhood gathering with voters who wanted to get to know us felt wonderfully cozy and comfortable. The big back door of the firehouse was up so that people could come in easily when they arrived on their way home from work. As I looked out, even the lighting seemed just right, with the sun setting on the short November day. The scene was quintessential New Hampshire and the personal interaction and open conversation quintessential John. Even the cold didn't bother me this time.

At one town hall a little later in New Hampshire, a woman got up to say that she had worn a silver bracelet during the Vietnam War in support of a soldier fighting there. Now she was wearing a black bracelet for her son who had given his life in Iraq. John talked about the war in Iraq at all his stops in New Hampshire, and explained why he supported the surge. He expected the bereaved mom to berate him for his position or blame him for her loss. But instead she took off the bracelet and held it out to him. She quietly asked John if he would wear it to remember his mission—and so that her son's sacrifice might not have been in vain. John got teary-eyed, but he managed to keep his composure.

"I would be honored to wear it, ma'am," he said. He took the bracelet and gave her a hug.

For the rest of that campaign and for the rest of his life, John wore the bracelet with the name of Matthew Stanley, who had died in Iraq at age twenty-two. When John died in 2018, we buried him with that bracelet. He always remembered the mission.

John won in New Hampshire. The next day, a big influx of donations came in from all over the country. The next couple of primaries went to Romney—and then it was time for South Carolina. I still had dark feelings from our experience in 2000, but John went all over the state meeting with voters. With nobody playing dirty in South Carolina this time, John's message did get out—well enough that he won. At the time, most of the Republican primaries were winner takes all, and now the momentum swung back to him. He got a big win in Florida, and with the back-to-back victories suddenly a lot of people wanted to board the Straight Talk Express. Governor Arnold Schwarzenegger endorsed John in California and Governor Rick Perry did the same in Texas. Then came Super Tuesday, when nearly half the country voted.

I joined John in Texas for Super Tuesday, knowing it could be make or break for his campaign. A big crowd of his supporters gathered in an arena that evening to cheer him on. John and I sat together with some staffers in a room backstage, and as the results rolled in and John's victories piled up, everyone got more and more excited. Everything feels bigger in Texas—so it seemed the perfect place to find out that John had enough delegates to win the nomination. When it was time for John to go out and make his victory speech, we held hands and walked through the tunnel leading to the stage. As the cheers from the crowd grew louder and closer, John stopped for a moment and squeezed my hand.

"Can you believe this?" he asked, his voice filled with joyous wonder. "How did we get here?"

"You got us here," I said.

He looked at me, and for a moment in the midst of the chaos and excitement and crowds, it was just the two of us.

We stepped out onto the stage, and I was glad that I had picked a yellow dress to wear for the evening—a happy nod to the yellow rose of Texas. Someone had hung a banner from one of the balconies with the delegate total, and I waved at them, my face breaking into a big smile. It was a great moment, the kind that you hope for your whole life. But when I remember that night now, the greatest joy I feel comes from that exchange in the tunnel—just John and me sharing a look, a love, and an understanding that the moment meant so much because we were in it together. When you come right down to it, even in the most public and visible moments of life, family is still all that really matters.

After that night, things happened fast. Romney bowed out and asked his delegates to back John. President Bush threw his support toward the campaign—and even though Bush was struggling with his own declining popularity at the time, he was still president and it meant something to us and his supporters. I was excited for John but still cautious. Jimmy had just started his first deployment in Iraq, and I worried every day that his dad's new prominence would make him a target. Jimmy himself stayed levelheaded. At one point long after, when he had finally come home safely, he told us that he had been digging in mud after a rainstorm in Anbar Province when one of his officers sought him out and let him know that his dad had won the New Hampshire primary. Jimmy listened to the news and nodded.

If he wondered what advantages that brought him, he didn't have to wait long to find out. "Keep digging," the sergeant said.

"Yes, sir," Jimmy replied, getting back to work.

John almost never talked publicly about Jimmy and Jack being in the military—he refused to get political gain from their honorable service. I stayed quiet for a different reason. I knew that any hints of where Jimmy was located could add to the danger of his service. The press, however, had no such concerns. During the general election, we heard that several outlets sent reporters to Iraq to try to find him. I don't know what they wanted to prove—maybe they thought the senator's son would be sitting in some cushy office far away from the action. It probably didn't occur to them—or at least I hope it didn't—that finding Jimmy would put him even further into harm's way. The Marines did understand, and I will be forever grateful for the casual but clever way they protected him.

From what I later heard, a crew from one network arrived in Anbar Province, having somehow learned that Jimmy was stationed there. There were many FOBs in the area, which is military short-hand for a local base. ("Forward operating base" is the technical name.) When the crew pulled up at FOB Gold, a Marine officer greeted them and said something like, "McCain isn't here. You might try FOB Emerald." The crew went thumping off to FOB Emerald, ten miles away, only to be told at the gate, "You might try FOB Silver." At the next stop, they encountered the same routine. And so on. The Marines ran the reporters all over Anbar Province and never let them know where Jimmy was actually stationed.

Hearing about their strategy made me laugh in gratitude and relief. When a producer from CNN told me about his experience trying to track down Jimmy, I asked a Marine officer if it sounded true. He gave a little nod. "Do you think a Marine would reveal the location of your son?" he asked solemnly. "No way, ma'am. No way."

My worry about Jimmy was also mingled with the admiration I

When we first got together, John had already spent five years as a POW in Vietnam and still served in the Navy. I knew I loved him but I had no idea he would spend the rest of his career in the political spotlight.

We had a storybook wedding in Phoenix in 1980, and the eighteen-year age gap between us didn't matter then—or ever.

We honeymooned in Hawaii, the place we met, and that launched my lifetime passion for travel.

Before I met John, I didn't plan on getting married. I liked being crowned Junior Rodeo Queen in the spring of 1969 and hanging out with my sorority sisters from Kappa Alpha Theta, here at Busch Gardens in 1975. *From left*—me, Nani Dalby Bush, Kathy McKee Buckingham.

My dad believed he could succeed at anything. He flew B-17s in the Air Force and then built up the largest beer distributorship in the West. He adored me and admired John, and I could talk to him about anything. Here we toasted the USC Father Daughter weekend in 1975.

John is the baby in the photo here, growing up in a tradition of honor and service. His father (left) and grandfather were both important Navy admirals, and the warship USS *John S. McCain* is named for all three generations of brave McCains.

We celebrated Roberta McCain's one hundredth birthday in 2012. John's mother was always strong and unflappable, and I learned so much from her about courage and the life of a military spouse. She remained stoic during John's funeral, and we finally lost her in 2020, at age 108.

I often got nervous on planes, so I decided to learn as much as I could about them. I ended up getting my pilot's license and buying this small plane, which I used to fly John all over the state for his first Senate race.

Congressman John McCain

John's political career took off at the same time that we were starting our family. During John's first Senate run, we attended many events holding Meghan and Jack (*above*), including in our family portrait on the Capitol steps (*below*).

John went to Hanoi with CBS News anchor Walter Cronkite in 1985, and his trip helped open up a diplomatic relationship between the United States and Vietnam. I hosted a party in Washington, D.C., in honor of Ronald Reagan's inauguration while John was away. As a politician's wife, you quickly learn to take things in stride.

At an orphanage in Bangladesh started by Mother Teresa, I first encountered our daughter Bridget. I always felt that she picked me as her mother. I brought her back to Arizona for medical help, but John and I immediately knew that we would never let her go.

John attended the Naval Academy, as did our son Jack, and it is an important part of the McCain legacy. We visited there during the 2000 presidential campaign.

Our ranch in northern Arizona was always our family getaway—the one place we could retreat for fun and outdoor living. It now holds bittersweet memories, because John spent the last months of his life there, teaching us all how to die with grace and courage.

John gave the commencement address at the Naval Academy in 1993. A graduate gave Jack his midshipman's cap, and Jack decided right then that he would eventually earn one of his own.

Having two sons in the military makes me very proud, but I had many moments of fear for their safety, too. When Jimmy left Camp Pendleton for his second deployment with the Marines in 2009 (*above*) I burst into tears. A happier moment came on Christmas morning 2010 (*below*) when Jack and John each donned their flight jackets.

Bridget and I share a moment at the 2008 Republican convention. During the South Carolina primary in 2000, the Bush campaign viciously slandered our daughter. It was one of the most painful experiences of my political life. No child deserves to be the target of lies and innuendo—and it remains the one bitter taste I have of political campaigns.

I visited Calcutta in 1994 and thanked Mother Teresa for all she had done—and for giving us Bridget.

I've always loved car racing, whether NASCAR or the Indy 500. Along with my son Jack, I got involved in drift racing, which was a little crazy and a very big thrill.

This baby was just born in the tent behind me. In 1991, I had a medical team in Iraq working with our army to help these folks, who were trying to get into Kuwait.

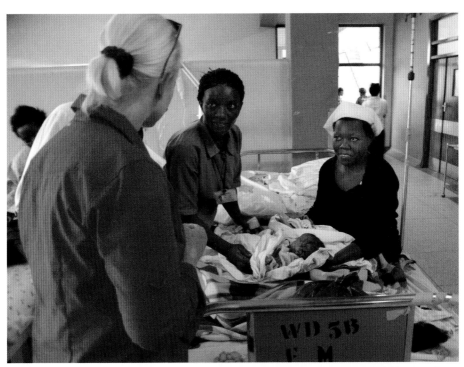

I visited the Democratic Republic of Congo many times, setting up field hospitals and otherwise trying to combat the unthinkable levels of poverty and hunger. We focused on helping the babies and children who were often undernourished and left as orphans when their parents were killed by violence.

When I visit refugee camps, I listen to the stories and try to figure out how I can make a difference. For me, philanthropy isn't about writing a check—it's about being on the ground and caring.

I always knew John was beloved, but I was overwhelmed by the number of leaders from around the world who attended his funeral at the Washington National Cathedral. Presidents Bush, Clinton, and Obama were there. Our longtime friend and now president Joe Biden gave a moving tribute to John at a more intimate service in Arizona that took place a few days before.

We were all so happy at Jack's wedding to Renee in 2013. As a major in the Air Force, she actually outranked him, and we were proud to get both a terrific daughter-in-law and a new branch of the military in our family.

felt toward him and the many other young men and women serving their country. So, even though I rarely made political statements of my own, I couldn't help reacting one day in February when Michelle Obama told a campaign event, "For the first time in my adult life, I am really proud of my country." For the first time in her life, really? I couldn't let that one pass by unnoticed. I had two sons in the military and a husband whose family had given generations of service. While introducing John at our next campaign rally, I made a point of saying that I was very proud of my country. Since I rarely got political in my own right, reporters pounced, asking if I meant that as a response to Michelle.

"I have and always will be proud of my country," I said firmly.

All of us get caught saying things awkwardly or having our words misinterpreted, and during a campaign you often end up explaining that what you said isn't what you meant to say. But I knew I wouldn't have to walk this one back. I was proud of my country, period. Michelle Obama had made her comment in Wisconsin, right before the state's primary. Barack had just won eight consecutive states over Hillary Clinton, and I suppose she meant to suggest her pride that Americans were casting votes for an African American. At rallies in Milwaukee and Madison, she couched the "finally proud of my country" comment by saying that "people are hungry for change" and "hope is finally making a comeback." Despite our complicated history in America with race relations, the bigger implication bothered me then, and it bothers me now. The brave military people I have met over many years show me that there has always been much to be proud of in America.

I knew that the press pack would be different in 2008 than it had been in our previous campaign, and a particular incident showed me just how crazy the twenty-four-hour news cycle had become. One day, I was on our plane going from one rally to another. In the back of the plane, I noticed two well-known reporters talking to each other. We landed and, barely twenty minutes later, one of the reporters was on camera describing information he received from "an unnamed source on the campaign." It took me a moment to realize that the source was . . . the other reporter. Under pressure to produce stories almost around the clock, even the best of journalists couldn't come up with something fresh and original every single day. But the need for new material meant that you never quite knew what small comment might get blown out of proportion.

At the beginning of September, delegates from every state would gather at the Republican National Convention to formally nominate John as the Republican presidential candidate. There were a thousand details to consider, from who would sing the national anthem to how many balloons would get released. Fortunately, most of the choices weren't mine to make—but I did get involved in the discussions about one matter. Before the convention, John needed to select a vice presidential candidate to add to the ticket. He and I talked about it often because we knew that any choice he made would be endlessly analyzed and second-guessed. The right choice could change the momentum of the race and give voters a new view of John. Political columnists, campaign advisers, and congressional colleagues all tossed around names to consider. I had my opinion, and John had his.

As it turned out, neither of us got our choice.

CHAPTER 9

In the Spotlight

The end of the primary season was a lot of fun, with big crowds and enthusiastic supporters eager to shake hands. John liked direct contact with voters, and he refused the Secret Service protection normally offered to candidates. I begged him to be safe and accept the protection, but he didn't even think about it. He wasn't making a point—it was just who he was. As John waded blithely into crowds, I often stayed slightly back, scanning the faces and looking for potential trouble. Sometimes as we were working rope lines, talking and shaking hands, I would get uncomfortable about certain people's weird behavior—but John would just laugh about it. In his mind, he could survive anything, and he didn't want black-suited men talking into their sleeves and following him around.

The Secret Service approached John several times, requesting to screen people arriving for his events, but he continued to resist. Then at a rally in Memphis, Tennessee, I saw a woman with a knife in her hand, trying to get closer. That night, when we got back to our hotel room, I packed my suitcase and headed to the door.

"Where are you going?" John asked.

"Home," I said. "You can get stabbed or killed if you want, but you're not taking me with you."

"You can't leave," John said.

"Oh, but I'm going," I said.

It wasn't an idle threat—threatening to leave was the only way I could get John to focus on the seriousness of the danger. We talked some more and he didn't budge in his position. I got my stuff, gave John a kiss goodbye, and got in a car to go to the airport. I was half-way there when John called me.

"I'm sorry. You're exactly right. Please come back."

I did. The next day, the Secret Service joined us. However wary John might have been, the agents' skill and competence quickly won him over. I had two security details—one led by a charming woman, and the other led by a friendly guy from Kentucky. Both were lovely, hardworking, and dedicated professionals.

"The one thing we don't do is carry luggage," one of the leads explained to me, somewhat apologetically, on the first day.

"I'm fine with that," I said. "You're here for us, and we'll play by your rules."

The Secret Service always uses code names for the people they protect, and John's was Phoenix—a reference both to his hometown and to the bird in Greek mythology that rises from the ashes. Everyone in the family gets a name that begins with the same first letter, and the original plan was for my code name to be Pilsner. When I heard about it later, I thought it was clever—a sly reference to my family's beer distributorship. But someone had apparently worried that I'd be offended and changed it to Parasol. Maybe they thought it fit my ladylike image. Or else they knew that I like to stay out of the sun.

The women and men in our detail worked around the clock, in rotations of two weeks on and two weeks off. I felt humbled that they were away from their families, protecting us around the clock, and I tried to show appreciation in even the smallest ways. When we stayed at the ranch, they had their own trailer, but I made sure we cooked for them, and I'd bring over beverages on a hot day. Out on the campaign trail, they got amped up a few times, warning us that they expected protestors or potential trouble at an event. Each time, John listened to the briefing and then said, "Okay, let's do it anyway." They'd come up with a plan that might involve a dummy car or a switch in entrances or one of many other things that we didn't even know about. I felt a great sense of relief and no longer worried about John venturing into huge crowds every day. Even if you're a hero like John McCain, you fly better when someone has your back.

John prided himself on being on time for everything—he ran a military clock in his head and he never kept people waiting. But one time we had a problem getting to an event in Miami, and we realized we would be nearly two hours late. The thought of showing up late was driving both of us crazy, and we half expected to find an empty hall—or at least irate voters—when we arrived. Instead, we walked into an arena filled with some twenty thousand people, many of them Cuban nationals, and all of them partying and laughing and dancing and singing. It was a Latin fiesta like we had never seen before. As we walked toward the stage, I felt a few pinches on my backside, but there was such joy in the room that it just made me laugh. When John started to talk, the people in the room were shouting their love and support. In politics, moments like that make the painful times worthwhile.

Once it became clear that John would be the nominee, speculation began about who his vice president might be. John would turn seventy-two just before the convention. Today, that doesn't seem like an advanced age at all, given the age of recent nominees. But winning in 2008 would have made John the oldest person elected president at the time. Some of his advisers had urged him earlier in the campaign to promise that he would run for only one term, as both a concession to his age and proof that he had gotten into the race to help the country, not advance his own ambition. I thought it was a terrible idea. In my view, you should never limit your options or try to guess the future. Whatever you're doing in life, come in with all the strength and power you can. After thinking it over, John agreed that he didn't want to start out as a lame-duck president, and he never made the promise. As it turned out, John could have served two full terms in excellent health and at high capacity before he died—still way too young—at age eighty-two.

Having been on a short list for vice president several times in his career, John knew that the selection often involved complicated calculations. Many nominees play a game of campaign geography, trying to figure out who could balance the ticket and help win the electoral college. John thought more about who would be a good partner for governing. One weekend, we invited several of John's friends to our cabin in Oak Creek for a get-together; the group included Mitt Romney and Jon Huntsman and several other people who John admired. As soon as the press saw the list, they immediately assumed it was a gathering of vice presidential contenders. Some of them might have been, but the weekend was really meant to be a time to connect with good friends over good food. Jimmy was just home from a tour in Iraq, and the conversation mixed politics with humor and goodwill. We had no interviews or VP discussions at all.

John wanted me involved in the real VP choice, and he bounced a lot of ideas off me. My decision was easy—I was for Joe Lieberman all the way. We had been friends with Joe for many years, and I particularly liked that he and John had huge respect for each other. They worked well together in the Senate, traveling frequently to trouble spots around the world to get firsthand knowledge of diplomatic situations. Both had strongly supported the surge in Iraq and considered the war on terror a national priority. Plus, Joe seemed to share John's sense of integrity above all else.

Joe had a complicated political history. First elected to the Senate in 1988 as a moderate Democrat from Connecticut, he became the vice presidential candidate in 2000 on the Gore-Lieberman ticket. Nobody would ever forget that messy election, since it ended up in the Supreme Court. Joe returned to the Senate afterward, but when he ran again for his seat in 2006, he lost the Democratic primary, probably as a result of his support for the Iraq War. Not one to quit, he created an independent party for himself and got 50 percent of the vote in the general election, overcoming both the Republican candidate and the Democrat who had beaten him in the primary. He went back to the Senate.

John and I both appreciated Joe's resolve. After 2006, he caucused with the Democrats but kept his independence when it came time to vote. In that way, he was just like John, who always cared about policy over party and believed in making alliances across the aisle. In keeping with those values, Joe took the unexpected step in 2008 of endorsing John for the presidency. He took his stance in New Hampshire, before the state's primary, saying simply that he thought John was the most qualified Republican to become president. When a reporter asked if he might end up as John McCain's running mate, Joe joked, "I think John has much better judgment than that."

As the convention neared and John thought more and more about his vice president, his good judgment leaned toward Lieberman. But then his advisers poured some cold water on his hot idea. The Republican Party had a right-wing core that didn't believe in working across the aisle at all. They were already a little suspicious of John for some of his cultural attitudes, and his advisers feared that they would block Lieberman and not let him through the convention. How could they nominate a Republican vice president who had already sought the same office as a Democrat?

A few months earlier, John had sat down with Sarah Palin, the governor of Alaska, and her husband, Todd, at the National Governors Association conference in Washington, D.C. "She's no-nonsense and they're a good, down-to-earth couple," John had told me at the time. Governor Palin had just had a baby, and it amazed me that she had made it to the conference at all. She was obviously resilient, and since she liked both kids and the outdoors, it was easy for me to relate to her.

Choosing Joe as a running mate would have been a gutsy move. If that was out, John still wanted to make a bold statement. With the convention just a couple of weeks away, his advisers got together and hashed out possibilities. They understood John's requirements, and they also wanted someone who might appeal to the outspoken right wing of the party. When they came back suggesting Palin, John liked the idea. He called her almost immediately for an interview.

We didn't want the press getting wind of the deliberations, so we made elaborate plans to avoid detection. We had Governor Palin fly from Alaska to Flagstaff, Arizona, where a friend of ours had a home. She stayed there overnight and then drove in a pickup truck to our cabin in Oak Creek. John and I sat down and talked to her together, and then we each met with her alone. You don't always have to like your running mate for it to be a good fit politically—but we did like her.

For our meeting, I took Governor Palin for a stroll around the grounds. Since she was clearly comfortable in the outdoors, I pointed out the plants and animals on the property that always delighted us. I thought she was charming and delightful and ambitious—just as a woman in her position should be. But she also struck me as naïve about national politics. As governor of Alaska, she had been in the public eye, but I wanted her to understand that at this level, the scrutiny would be completely different. We sat down with cups of tea, and I expressed concern about her five children, including the baby, Trig, who had just been born with Down syndrome.

"You're a young family, and this would be a huge undertaking," I told her. "It will have a bigger effect on everyone's daily life than you can begin to imagine."

She nodded, and we talked for a while about dealing with family issues. Their older son was thinking about the Army at that point, and she asked me what it was like to have a son in combat. She didn't mention any concerns about having her daughters' lives examined by the media. We talked about the time and commitment a campaign would take, but she said she'd dealt with the same thing when she ran for governor.

"We have a lot of territory to cover in Alaska, too," she said.

After meeting with Sarah, John and I conferred with his advisers. I was probably the most reluctant to go ahead. I wanted what was best for my husband, and I wasn't sure she fit the bill—but I trusted him to make the decision. He wanted to make an outside-the-box choice and not go with another white male. With Barack Obama, the Democrats had a charismatic leader who stood for forward-looking ideas. John wanted someone who would reinforce his own ambition to run as a figure of change. When the press attacked Palin later for her lack of experience and hazy policy positions, John took full responsibility and never, ever blamed her.

"She didn't put herself on the ticket," John explained. "I did."

Ultimately it was our decision. We made what we thought was the best choice at the time and stood by it.

We flew to Ohio to make the announcement. John had a great speech prepared describing Sarah Palin as the right partner for him and promising that she had the "grit, integrity, good sense, and fierce devotion to the common good" that was needed in Washington. It was an incredibly hot and humid day, and Sarah had her whole family with her. Meghan McCain has the best radar of anyone I know. She took one look at Bristol, who was holding both baby Trig and a very heavy blanket in front of her stomach, and she immediately got the whole situation.

"The older daughter is pregnant, Mom, in case you didn't know that," Meghan said when we came off the stage after the announcement.

"Oh, come on, Meghan, no she's not. Sarah would have mentioned it," I said.

"Trust me. She's pregnant," Meghan said. "That's what's going on with her."

John and I rolled our eyes at Meghan being dramatic again. But this time, as often happened, she was completely right. The team we had sent to vet the Palins hadn't come back with that information. But who would ever think to ask if a seventeen-year-old was pregnant? I thought back to my conversation with Palin at the cabin. I thought we'd had an open and thoughtful discussion of family, so it was mind-boggling to think that she never mentioned that her seventeen-year-old daughter Bristol was pregnant. I'm a mom, and our family is pro-life! As a parent, you love your children and support them in any circumstances. Did she think that John wouldn't make an offer if she were up-front about the situation?

To most reporters outside Alaska, Sarah Palin was a new figure. After the announcement, they pounced to find out everything they could about her and her family. At first it was all interest and excitement—but then the press started going after Palin in a manner that was completely unconscionable. They talked about her clothes, about her kids, about her pregnant daughter and whether she would marry her boyfriend. They speculated—based on nothing—whether Trig was actually Bristol's child, not Sarah's. Talking about a candidate and a spouse is one thing, but the press attacked the Palin children in a way that was wrong and unfair. Children don't ask to be part of a campaign. They should be off-limits. I felt terrible about how Bristol was treated. I had tried hard to warn Sarah that day at the cabin about ramifications for her family, but she was eager to get on board. It's one thing to say "Yes, I want to do this," and another to actually live through the experience.

We knew from the beginning that Sarah wouldn't be completely up to speed on international issues, but that was already John's area of expertise, and we had people to help her learn. When we flew to events together, John would sit with her on the airplane and provide background and perspective on key global issues. She had the best teacher in the world in him.

In the beginning, we had the sense that things were going okay. Sarah drew huge crowds at her events, and John loved the attention she got. Really, he loved it. I think some candidates might have worried if their No. 2 was getting the No. 1 amount of press and awareness, but he was delighted. Then some of her inexperience started becoming more and more apparent.

The staffers responsible for Palin's schedule decided to set up just a few interviews with select reporters. One of those reporters was Katie Couric—and that interview turned out to be a prime-time disaster. Afterward, some people thought that Couric had always intended to embarrass Sarah, but there is simply no way to excuse the rambling and disjointed answers the vice presidential nominee gave. Asked about a potential Bush administration bank bailout, Palin gave a tortured and garbled reply that made no sense at all. When asked what newspapers and magazines she read, she couldn't name one. She was also hazy on why she made a point of saying that Alaska was near Russia. When actress Tina Fey parodied the interview on *Saturday Night Live*, she didn't have to make anything up. She just used the answers verbatim. People wondered why Palin seemed so unprepared, and the answer is simple. She didn't want to take direction from John's team or sit down for any mock interviews in preparation.

She believed in her own abilities. Confidence is great—but only when it's warranted.

Despite the concerns about her performance and the merciless criticism in the press, John took it in stride. "We'll get through this," he said.

I wanted Sarah to do better, but I also thought she had been unfairly skewered by the press. She was a woman and an outsider in political Washington, and I don't think an insider male would have been similarly dumped on.

The campaign schedule often had me appearing with Todd Palin at events, and I enjoyed getting to know him. Our first joint event was in Los Angeles at a Republican group called Friends of Abe—as in Abraham Lincoln. The group had been started just a few years earlier by some conservative Hollywood celebrities. Fairly secretive, they kept their membership list closed, and neither fans nor reporters could just walk into an event. While a few well-known stars of the time like Kelsey Grammer, Jon Voight, and Gary Sinise proudly flaunted their Republican ideology, many others preferred to keep their political positions quiet. Being a conservative doesn't necessarily play well in Hollywood. We recognized a lot of people in the audience, and they all loved Todd immediately. He is understated but a lot of fun—and definitely the outdoorsy guy everyone wants to have a beer with.

Todd and I continued to appear at town halls and rotary clubs around the country, and he was utterly gracious and kind to me. It was fun spending time together. He came across as a guy just trying to help his wife, and I think that's exactly what he was. I always thought he would rather be home fishing in Alaska, but he stayed cheerful and friendly and gave his all to the campaign. I appreciated that.

I knew that my biggest moment in the spotlight would be the speech I gave at the Republican convention. I've made a lot of speeches in my life, but I couldn't stop thinking about the fact that tens of millions of people would tune in to watch this one. I had spent many years wanting to be perfect for John, and now I really had to be. Preparing for that speech was the most challenging and nerve-racking experience of the campaign. For some thirty years, I had known John McCain as a husband, father, and friend, and I wanted the world to see the same honorable, kind, funny, and compassionate man I did. I wanted to do it right—and like John, I wanted to do it my way.

Most convention speeches are given from behind a lectern, but I was talking as a mom and a wife, not a politician. I had the feeling that I should step out from behind the lectern and talk directly to the audience. It's much easier to stand in one place and read from the teleprompter, but if I could walk and talk and really connect with the audience, maybe I could reach them on a more personal level.

Two people were helping me write the speech, and I told them the themes that were important to me. I wanted to both humanize myself as a mom who had watched a son go into combat, and help everyone see John as an incredible leader who cared about families and would keep America strong and secure. We had to give an advance copy of the script to the press corps, and there would be teleprompters to back me up. But because the words were coming from my heart, I didn't want to look like I was reading. I spent many hours practicing what I would say. Some of my old anxieties crept back, and I struggled with the fear of letting John down. I knew that any flub I made would reflect badly on him and not be forgotten, but I'd finally reached a point where I refused to let apprehension and worry consume me. I reminded myself that the greatest strides in life come when you accept challenges and push yourself to your limits. It can be scary, and your instinct may be to back off and go the easy route. But that means giving up before you start—and McCains don't do that.

The convention began on Monday, September 1, 2008, the same

day a hurricane hit parts of the United States after pounding Haiti and Cuba, causing devastating damage. President Bush decided to cancel his first-night speech and stay in Washington. I took the stage with Laura Bush to make a short appeal for humanitarian aid and help for hurricane victims. The topic was important to me and so in keeping with the aid work I had done my whole life that I felt comfortable addressing the huge hall of delegates. But the real test would come when I gave my full address on Thursday.

Conventions are loud and raucous, and by Thursday, the enormous crowd was primed and ready. I would give my speech—and then John would accept the nomination of his party. I walked out onto the stage with the seven McCain children to wild cheering and applause. Jimmy and Jack were on either side of me, their arms linked through mine. I saw a crush of people waving signs with my name and WE LOVE CINDY! written on them. It's overwhelming and a bit humbling to get that kind of reception. Our extended family all stood together, feeling the pride and family connection that John had inspired. When the cheering calmed down, I introduced each of the children, who then hugged me and walked back to their seats. I launched my speech by saying that nothing in my life had made me happier or more fulfilled than being a mother. When you start with the truth, the rest is easy.

Well, not easy. The first few minutes of a speech are the most challenging, because your heart is pounding. I took a breath and reminded myself to relax and smile. *Remember, you're talking about your husband—the man you love, respect, and admire. How hard can that be?* Sure enough, within a couple of minutes, I got into a rhythm where I wasn't just saying the words, I was feeling them. I talked about my sons' military service, the lifelong example of honesty and self-sacrifice that John had set, and his unwavering devotion to his country. I talked about my own dad and how all of us have a duty to nurture the next generation. When I finished, the audience stood and cheered, and our family rushed up to rejoin me onstage. In that moment, I felt a great surge of joy. Whatever the press said about my speech wouldn't matter. I had done what I needed to do and said what was in my heart.

Coming out of the convention on September 4, 2008, polls showed John leading by eight or so points. But eleven days later, on September 15, the investment bank Lehman Brothers collapsed. The federal government had refused to bail the company out, as it had done with other struggling banks, and that decision unleashed a financial collapse that reached from Wall Street to Main Street before spreading around the world. The Bush administration tried to take steps to stop the panic and staunch the crisis, but President Bush was in the White House, and voters reasonably enough blamed him as they watched their stocks tumble and savings disappear. His popularity was at an all-time low. John was a very different Republican than Bush, but he still got much of the reflected blame.

After the long primary season and the convention, you have just two months of campaigning before the general election. It feels like both the longest time imaginable and the shortest. We crisscrossed the country more times than I could count, and our days were endlessly packed. When we visited big states like Pennsylvania, Michigan, or Ohio, there were too many people for a single candidate to meet. So the schedule often had me doing events separate from John. I enjoyed the speeches and the crowds, but after being apart for several days in a row, I always felt glad when John and I got back together.

One particular evening when we reunited, I realized something was off. John hadn't had enough sleep, he hadn't eaten right, and since he was tired, he was at the end of his tether. John's quick temper was his one much-discussed shortcoming, and I knew he could blow the whole campaign with an ill-timed flare-up. I told his team that was it—I had to stay with John no matter what, just to make sure he stayed healthy and okay. I didn't mind taking on that traditional spouse's role. I was juggling a lot of duties that were important in their own right, but nothing was more important than traveling with John to keep things sane. I could distract him with talk about the children, and I could also intervene when he needed a break. John loved talking to people and never wanted to let anyone down, so he made a habit of staying at events until the last handshake. Usually he had enough energy to outlast everybody, the press corps included, but I could tell when the time had come to wrap up the photo line.

The days were long and wearying. The schedule was supposed to be twelve hours on and then twelve hours off, but it didn't always work out that way. Sometimes we'd have days that stretched to eighteen hours. Unless I had an event in the evening that required a formal dress, I'd put on one outfit in the morning and wear it all day, sometimes to six different events. Men rarely have to worry about what they wear, but for women, it's always a double-edged sword. If you look too good and put together, you get criticized as an ice queen who spends too much on clothes. But if you look less than perfect, there's nasty harping and whispers of "What's the matter with her?"

We traveled with hair and makeup people because you have to look perfect for every public appearance. Women who have busy days know how hard it is to find the outfit that you'll be comfortable wearing from morning until night. I've always worn classic clothes that travel well and are comfortable—I'm not a ruffles and frills kind of gal. I usually wore a simple dress with clean, sophisticated lines, and often put a jacket over it. Expectations for political spouses had eased a little by then, so I could also get away with wearing turtlenecks and more casual outfits when the occasion allowed. But heels were still de rigueur. I wore them every day, for hours on end. For two years after the race, I refused to put on another pair of high heels.

For the convention speech, I chose an Oscar de la Renta dress because the style and colors were flattering on me. One reporter said

that my outfit cost $300,000. When I first heard that, I laughed—
she had overshot the real price by a couple of zeroes. But somehow
the number stuck.

Campaigns can be dizzying and exhausting because of all the
information and points of view coming at you. You have to learn what
to take in, what to filter out, and how to shut off the noise at the end
of the day. Some of the political pundits framed the campaign as pitting John McCain's experience versus Barack Obama's call for change.
Others argued that the selection of Sarah Palin undercut John's
advantage on the experience side. How could he allow someone so
unworldly to be a heartbeat from the presidency? Eventually, we
stopped listening to the pundits. Instead of watching the news when
we went back to our hotel room every night, John would turn on
ESPN and I'd plug into my iPod. Sometimes we would review the
day, but mostly we took advantage of having a few hours away from
the noise.

The three McCain-Obama debates were eye-opening for me.
Onstage the candidates look calm and in control, but what goes on
before and after is completely wild. The candidates arrive with big
contingents, and the opposing mobs check each other out. It always
made me think of packs of dogs circling around and sniffing one
another. I heard a lot of arguing among the staffers about positioning
and who was sitting where. *Who gets seen from this camera angle, and
who's in the shot from that one? Where on the stage will the candidates
shake hands?* As Shakespeare said in a different context, it's a lot of
sound and fury signifying nothing.

Arriving for one debate with John and our team, I met Michelle
Obama for the first time. Despite my objection to the comment she
had made earlier in the campaign, she's a strong, smart, and lovely
woman, and a wonderful mom and wife. If we had met in a personal
situation, we probably would have liked each other. It would have
been nice to be able to support and commiserate about our

experiences on the campaign trail, but we were coming in as part of two opposing camps, which made it more difficult. When you're totally wrapped up in the moment, the circus surrounding the debate makes real conversation unlikely.

The debates were competitive, but without any nastiness or venom. John always wanted people to see that his concern was the country, not himself. He suspended his campaign briefly in September to go back to Washington after the historic financial crash. He thought it was the right thing to do, so we were all surprised when the suspension was made to seem like a political maneuver. All John could do was stick to his principles. He put out a joint statement with Obama urging Democrats and Republicans in Congress to rise above politics and take action.

For John, those weren't just words. At a town hall the next month, he disagreed with a man who said that he was afraid of Obama. John countered that he respected Obama's accomplishments and asked that everyone be respectful, "because that's the way politics should be conducted in America." Shockingly, there were boos from his partisan supporters. But he stuck with his honorable approach later in the rally, when a woman stood up and said she couldn't trust Obama and, struggling to explain why, called him an Arab. John shook his head and took the microphone away from her. "No, ma'am. He's a decent family man, a citizen that I just happen to have disagreements with." He went on to explain, "If I didn't think I'd be a heck of a lot better president, I wouldn't be running. And that's the point."

That *is* the point. You can believe in yourself and ask others to follow you without tearing down your opponents. Given the viciousness, bullying, and attack-dog tactics that defined later campaigns, many people look back at 2008 and John's response at that town hall as the last hurrah of dignified campaigning. I wouldn't disagree. But this is still the same America that John believed in, and maybe we can conduct politics the way John did once again. It requires all of us to take a step back and listen to ideas rather than threats. We also need to be savvier about who we follow. My advice is to look for the person in either party who has a reasoned voice—and ignore those who focus on getting attention for themselves.

After the Katie Couric interview, some Republicans saw Sarah Palin as a liability to the ticket. There were even calls for her to resign. Palin was a strong campaigner, though, and continued to draw crowds. She prepared hard for her vice presidential debate against Joe Biden, and while she did fine, most people called it a victory for Biden. Between the Palin problem and the financial crisis, John's lead started to slip away. At some point, I sensed that we weren't going to get it back—but when you have thousands of people working for you and millions planning to vote for you, you have to keep giving your all every single day. One day as we went to an event with a huge crowd of cheering people waving signs for McCain-Palin, John stopped and smiled at me.

"Let's appreciate these moments," he said. "We won't have them forever."

"You're right," I said. "Whatever happens, we'll always remember this."

I watched in awe as people shook John's hand and started to cry at the honor of meeting him. People truly believed in what he could do—and I did, too.

On election night, we gathered with a big crowd in Phoenix and were fully prepared when the election results came in. The biggest glitch in the night was when we heard that Sarah Palin planned to commandeer the stage and give her own concession speech—something unheard of from a running mate. A couple of John's top aides went into her room to tell her that the speech she had already put into the teleprompter was a no-go and she needed to have some respect for good manners, courtesy, and protocol. We heard afterward that she was furious—but so were we.

By then, many political observers had suggested that Palin cost John the election. She alienated a lot of swing voters who otherwise liked John, and she undermined his appeal as the wise, experienced candidate. No one factor ever determines an election, but do I think John might have been president if not for her? Yes, I do.

John gave a brilliant concession speech that night, and I was blown away by the dignity he showed, his respect for the people and the process, and his recognition of President Obama's history-making win. We had been inside the campaign bubble for months—and suddenly that popped. After the speech, we said goodbye to the Secret Service agents who had become like family, and headed back to our own home.

"Do you happen to have keys?" John asked as we approached the house.

"No, I haven't had keys in months," I said. "Do you?"

"Nope."

We both laughed and laughed—releasing all the tension of the night. The Secret Service had always been there first and taken care of all access. Now, after months on the road, we were coming home. But getting back in wasn't going to be easy.

PART THREE

---⊗⊗⊗---

The Power of Caring

CHAPTER 10

Inaugurating a Future

The morning after the election, John and I unearthed our house and car keys from where they had been tucked away the past few months. We walked to Starbucks—our morning ritual before the campaign—and ate a leisurely breakfast at home in Phoenix. It was the first time we hadn't rushed in months. Then we got into the car and drove to our ranch in northern Arizona. It was the one place where we felt free to laugh and play, and John instinctively knew that a few days there would help us regain our spirits.

Being at the top of a presidential ticket is like being inside a bubble. You're with the same people every day on an airplane, inside a bus, in a meeting. It's not reality, but having spent the previous two years constantly surrounded by people, we weren't quite ready to be completely alone. Jack left immediately to return to the Naval Academy and Bridget had school, but Jimmy had been given a weeklong leave from the Marines for the election, so he had a few days left to be with us at the ranch. Meghan came with some of her closest circle, too, and we invited some other friends and key advisers. We never said it out loud, but John and I both understood that it would be important to have some activity around us.

We spent the long weekend relaxing and enjoying the outdoors and not talking (too much) about the campaign. John loved standing over a grill, so we spent our time barbecuing, enjoying one another's company, and barbecuing some more. The few days went by quickly, and on Sunday we went back to Phoenix. From there, John took off and went straight back to Washington. He never missed a beat, and he wanted to get back to work. I certainly understood that he had a job and he took it seriously. But after he left and the campaign staffers were gone and our kids and their friends went back to their lives, I felt a little lost. What was I supposed to do now?

Not that I sat around moping, but I did feel out of sorts. I tried not to spend a lot of time thinking about what might have been—or to blame myself for everything that had gone wrong. Could I have said or done something that would have led to a different outcome? The obvious answer was no, but part of your role as a wife and mother is to make things work out. When someone you love gets upset, you feel like you've failed.

It helped knowing that John had refused to be divisive and kept his honor and integrity throughout the campaign. If you participate in the kind of viciousness that has been the hallmark of so many recent presidential campaigns, I've always thought that you must feel a hollowness afterward. When you spend months spewing venom and hatred into the ether, those negative words and feelings eat at you and change who you are. Fortunately, we had done none of that.

President-elect and Mrs. Obama responded by being gracious and kind. The night before the inauguration, they hosted a large dinner party in honor of John and me, inviting our friends and campaign advisers. It was a classy thing to do and a remarkable celebration of bipartisanship. John and I arrived with our son Jack, who was dressed in his uniform from the Naval Academy, and John's outspoken mother, Roberta, then ninety-six years old and going strong. The four of us were asked to wait in a foyer for the president-elect to arrive. The door was open and the room was getting chilly, and Roberta started becoming aggressively agitated. Why did we have to wait and wait? And couldn't someone turn up the heat? Finally, President Obama walked through the door and greeted us. John shook his hand, as did I. We introduced our son Jack and my mother-in-law.

"I've heard all about you," the president said to Roberta.

"I bet you have," Roberta said. She peered at him and then gestured toward John and Jack. "I want you to know these two men are the real heroes here for serving their country."

She didn't say it in any rude way—just in a Roberta McCain way, which was always to be blunt and straightforward.

My style is a little more circumspect, so I thought, *Oh heavens!*

But President Obama took it in stride. "You should be very proud of them," he said, giving her a warm smile.

We all headed into the dinner, and waiting for us was a roomful of McCainiacs—our fond name for the people who had worked so hard for John during the campaign. Many in the close band of McCainiacs had been with him through many elections and become our good friends. It was touching, now, to see them in this setting. The president-elect greeted everyone and we were struck by his graciousness. Even though we would have preferred to win, all of us in the room understood that the country would be in the hands of an honorable man.

The next day, John and I went to the swearing-in ceremony in front of the U.S. Capitol. An enormous crowd had gathered to watch, stretching the entire length of the National Mall. It was the largest audience ever for an event in Washington, D.C., and the size of the crowd has never been matched. Tickets to the ceremony, which are distributed for free, were being scalped for thousands of dollars. I knew it would be a tough day for John, but as we walked together through the massive crowd, he set the tone for the day.

"We're here to support the country and the decision the voters have made," John said.

"You'll be okay?" I asked him.

"I'm feeling positive and hopeful," he said.

I nodded and decided that I would follow his cue.

During the inauguration ceremony, members of the Senate all sit together on the podium, on the vaulted seats that go high up behind the platform. The section gets packed with ambassadors, dignitaries, and foreign leaders, so the senators' spouses sit separately. I had long ago gotten used to being apart from John at official events, but this time I wished we could be together, holding hands or exchanging glances. I told myself that I should be close by to support him—but in truth, I desperately wanted him near to help *me* get through. In some ways, events like these are always hardest on the spouses. The person you love has been left disappointed—and there is absolutely nothing you can do to change the outcome. John still had his Senate seat, so he could always express his views and respond later to anything he disagreed with in the new administration. As a spouse, though, you generally just have to sit quietly and take it. And so I did.

After the inauguration, John stayed in Washington to resume his life as a senator and I flew home to Phoenix. Wandering through our condo, I felt a little shaky. I knew the active part of my life wasn't over, but I wasn't sure where I wanted to put my efforts next. Much of the previous two decades had been focused on raising my children and supporting John in his political life. I had my friends and my extensive volunteer work, but children and politics had stood as the key priorities. Now the kids were independent, and the furious excitement of campaigning had come to an abrupt halt. Imagine if you've been a working mom your whole life and then your kids go off to college and you lose your job, all in the same weekend. That's how I felt.

A lot of women struggle with reinventing themselves. They leave positions as teachers, CEOs, or even professional tennis players, and have to stop and think: What now? I also know many stay-at-home moms who have scrambled to find new meaning and direction after their children grew up or went off to college. Either way, it helps to talk to other people who have been in your situation.

When I found myself flailing, I gave a call to my friend Hadassah Lieberman, wife of Joe. She had campaigned hard for the Gore-Lieberman ticket in 2000, and the prolonged conclusion of that election must have left her feeling fully disoriented. For weeks, while the Florida recount battle went on, she didn't know if she would soon be moving to Number One Observatory Circle in Washington, D.C.—the official residence of the vice president—or returning to Connecticut.

"What did you do after it was all over?" I asked when we chatted on the phone. "How did you handle it?"

"I just went back home," she said. "All I can remember is that I sat around and ate for about a year."

"I know what you mean. I'm treating Cheetos as a key food group," I said.

We both laughed, but then she turned serious.

"People say, 'I can understand what you must be going through,' but they can't understand at all," she said. She pointed out that we were part of a very small sorority (and even smaller fraternity) of people who had supported their spouses through national campaigns.

"You're going to be in a different position now than you were before. All the great volunteer work you've done can be taken to a whole new level," she said.

It was a nice perspective, and I appreciated Hadassah's frank advice—that I now had a chance to use my name recognition for good. I just needed to get back into the swing of things and figure out where I was headed with the human rights issues that I'd always cared about. I surely would have managed it eventually, but I might have spent an extra couple of months eating Cheetos if I didn't get a call out of the blue from a celebrity who shared my global passions.

One morning, I answered my phone and someone said, "Hi, this is Ben Affleck." I assumed it was a joke. Which one of my kids or friends was pulling a prank on me? Ashton Kutcher's *Punk'd* had been a popular show on MTV the previous few years, so maybe they were doing it now with a political twist. I figured I'd play along for a little bit. I talked with whoever was pretending to be the popular movie star for a few minutes, and then it struck me. This wasn't one of my kids' friends or an MTV prankster. It really was Ben Affleck.

Most people know Ben Affleck as a Hollywood star. Along with Matt Damon, he wrote and starred in the Oscar-winning movie *Good Will Hunting* when they were both quite young. Affleck went on to make dozens of other movies, including *Pearl Harbor*, *Daredevil*, and *Gone Baby Gone*, working variously as an actor, writer, director, and producer. He has three children with his former wife, Jennifer Garner, and the tabloids can't get enough coverage of him as a dad and Hollywood man about town.

But Affleck was calling me about a subject far, far from Hollywood. He had grown passionate about the humanitarian crisis in the Democratic Republic of Congo, a place I had visited and where I had tried to help before. Ten years after war broke out, the country continued to be ravaged by violence and misrule. Children were forced to be soldiers, and an unthinkable level of poverty and hunger was rampant. One in five children died before the age of five. Affleck had visited a few times and was shocked and moved by what he saw. Wanting to call attention to the vast problems in the region, he had done a film for the United Nations and reported a segment for ABC television. Now he was starting a nonprofit called the Eastern Congo Initiative, and he had already attracted some high-profile donors to his cause. However shattered the Congo seemed, he believed that the people themselves remained strong and could find solutions. They just needed a chance.

"Look, I want you to join our organization," he said. "I need you to work with me on issues in eastern Congo. You understand it, you've been there, you've lived it. We can do a lot of good work together."

"We probably could," I agreed.

"Then you'll think about it?" he asked.

"I don't need to think about it," I said. "I'm all in."

"That's great! Do you want to get started right now?" he asked, only half joking.

"You bet I do!" I said with a laugh.

I was grateful for the phone call. His invitation was a catalyst for me to start focusing again on issues that had always moved me. In no time at all, I was on a plane to the Congo and heading back to work.

The eastern Congo is a difficult part of the world. Our work there had been focused in the city of Goma, which is on the border with Rwanda. In the 1990s, a horrific genocide in Rwanda by Hutu extremists against the ruling Tutsi minority left hundreds of thousands of people dead and led to an ongoing civil war. When the Tutsis retook the capital in 1994, some two million Hutus fled across the border. The refugee camps in Goma were overwhelmed. There wasn't enough food or water, and a cholera epidemic killed even more people than died of starvation. In the next few years, the Congo became mired in two wars, pitting Hutu against Tutsi, and the government led by Joseph Mobutu against the Rwanda-backed rebel movement that installed Laurent Kabila as president.

At the time, I was running the American Voluntary Medical Team. Our organization had a strong reputation. When there was a flare-up or problem around the world we would get a call—often from Geneva, where so many aid organizations are located: "We need your help. Can you be there?" Our answer was always yes. We would rally and get all our gear together. We were mobile and quick; once we arrived, we could set up a field hospital in under an hour.

We did that in Rwanda during the upheaval in the mid-1990s. We got a call to come help and I immediately said yes. The situation was tumultuous and the information emerging from the region vague at best. I arrived more eager than informed. We landed on an airstrip on the border of Rwanda and Congo (then called Zaire), and it was total chaos. It didn't take long to realize how dangerous our situation might be. On the Rwandan side, people were literally hacking each other to death. The callousness of the genocide was hard to fathom. But we pushed on.

We set up our hospital on the ground-floor of an old hotel. Other relief organizations from around the world were there, and we worked side by side to aid the refugees and to fight the huge cholera outbreak that was sweeping through the area. The level of chaos and human suffering reached almost unimaginable levels, and we focused on helping the babies and children. Many were undernourished, and others had become orphans when their parents were killed or died of illness.

The World Food Program came in to help with food shortages—each time their trucks showed up, a palpable tension filled the air. People were desperate for nourishment, but along with the hope of relief came the likelihood of terrible riots. They erupted again and again as groups of men rushed in, often toting weapons, to seize the aid packages and hoard them for the rebel leaders or military. The local people in need were left bereft, or sometimes dead.

One day after we'd been working for a while, I unwittingly waded into the midst of a food riot. It was terrifying. I had gone to a food distribution area with a couple of other people from AVMT in order to get some of the World Food Program provisions and bring them back to the hospital. We were waiting in a crowd, and the next thing I knew, some rebel men had swarmed in and began stabbing wildly, trying to get at the food sacks. I heard hysterical screaming, and then a crush of people pushing and panic all around. Standing right in the middle of the mayhem, I climbed on top of a nearby truck to get away. Rationally I knew that nobody wanted to hurt me; they wanted the food. But rationality doesn't play much part in a riot, and the rebels would unthinkingly cut down anybody in their way. My colleagues scrambled up next to me and then we made a quick plan for a wild run—and we escaped the mob. I was grateful to get away, but even after we stopped running and stood panting to catch our breath, I felt incredibly frustrated. We had ventured all this way and now had to leave without having gotten any food or supplies for the patients who needed it.

I returned to the Congo a couple of times after that—because how could I not? Seeing the depth of suffering made me want to do something. I always tried to work with relief groups that understood the local issues. I got a call from the organization ONE in 2008, asking me to join them on a trip to Rwanda and the Congo. The group is led by Bono, the lead singer of U2 and a leading activist in the global fight against poverty.

My schedulers assumed I would say no, because we were in the midst of that 2008 primary season. I was traveling constantly, speaking at events on John's behalf. How was I supposed to squeeze in a trip to Africa? But the more I thought about it, the more tempting it sounded. I cared so deeply about the work being done in the region, and the purpose of the trip was to meet people on the ground and gain a broader view of the issues they faced. Yes, I was bone-tired from campaigning, but going to Africa sounded far preferable to the personal nonsense I was experiencing during the presidential run.

At the time, one reporter had been fussing in print about how thin I was and speculating whether I could be anorexic. No, I was not. I just stayed so busy running around with the campaign that I didn't have time to eat. The charge bothered me because I believe women need a healthy body image—and I'd like to be a role model for that. But in the face of the true food problems in Africa, I could put it aside as so much silliness. You know you've reached a state of true emotional exhaustion when riding on bumpy roads and wondering where to find clean water can sound like a relief.

I went. As always on my trips to Africa, I met extraordinary people who were trying to solve the seemingly intractable problems of their country. They maintained a fierce optimism despite having seen extreme violence and the near collapse of their state. I thought about how connected the world is and how much we owe one another. For each of us, whatever we're going through can loom like an unconquerable mountain, and you gain so much when you step back and try to see your concerns from a distance. You start to understand what Humphrey Bogart means at the end of *Casablanca* when he tells a stunned Ingrid Bergman, "The problems of three little people don't amount to a hill of beans in this crazy world."

I think each of us can make a difference in this crazy world, but it was important that I approach John's campaign with a bigger perspective and a clearer head. When I came back from Africa, I knew that it didn't really matter if a reporter wanted to follow me around with a scale or if someone thought the outfit I was wearing cost too much (or maybe not enough). I knew that one way or another, I could overcome pettiness and find ways to do good.

. . .

There is so much need in the world and so many causes that deserve our attention, it can be difficult for any of us to know where to put our efforts. My approach to giving has always been to focus on issues that resound in my heart. I serve best when I have an almost visceral response to a problem. I had that reaction in the Congo when I walked into the refugee crisis the first time, and I felt it again when I went back with Ben Affleck.

Landing in the Congo this time, a few months after the 2008 election, felt both comfortable and strange. As with many visits, the goal was to talk with leaders and gain firsthand knowledge of the country's needs. Most of the time when you travel, you can find something that feels familiar. People are people, and no matter what their customs or current situation, their needs and desires cross country lines. But arriving in the Congo always makes me feel like I have landed in the middle of a scene from a movie. This time trucks rumbled through the streets of Goma, each one packed with rebels holding rocket-propelled grenade launchers straight up. Supplies were hard to come by and fear was palpable. The city had become so dangerous that we were advised to stay closer to the border where we could flee to Rwanda—which by then had reinvented itself into a peaceful, stable country—in an emergency.

Arriving in the Congo after a long flight, I went to our spartan lodging near the border. I would have liked to jump into a shower, but the hot water worked only occasionally and the very small towels I found didn't look too appealing. With its tiny bed and rickety dresser, the room made a Motel 6 look like the Ritz. But the people running it were nice and trying their best, and I realized that I was glad to be here. When I really care about a cause, I want to be on the ground, meeting the people and trying to understand the complexities of the situation, and this was the place to do it.

I opened the one carry-on bag I had brought and changed into my field clothes: pants that I could wash out in a creek if I had to, a lightweight shirt, and work boots. As I wiped some African dust off my windowsill, I thought of the American reporters during the campaign who liked to portray me as the standoffish rich lady who never got her hands dirty.

Ben was also on the ground, and I admired him for that. Like me, he didn't believe in checkbook charity. He got involved. When we met up the first day, he said, "I'm grateful that you're here. I know you can help open some doors."

"I can usually get a foot in," I said.

Together we met various local chiefs and officials, the people who needed to give us implicit permission to work in their areas. But as it turned out, Ben was able to make inroads that I couldn't. He got in to see Joseph Kabila, who had taken over as head of the country in 2001 after his father, Laurent, was assassinated. The Congo then adopted a constitution and elected Kabila to his first official term as president in 2006, but it would be a stretch to say that the country had embraced democracy. In a pattern that we have seen too often, in countries both distant and close to home, Kabila used the presidency to enrich himself and his own family. The corruption made international alliances more difficult.

Kabila never met with me. He liked the idea of talking with an American male movie star, but a blond female wasn't worth his time. The members of Kabila's government were curious about Ben's interest in their country, so they took meetings with him and would listen to his ideas on topics like aid to women and creating jobs through community-based programs. Many organizations found it difficult to work in the Congo, so I was impressed that Ben was able to talk with Kabila and get his input before making decisions.

Ben also had a warm relationship with Paul Kagame, the president of Rwanda, and one night, we went to his house for dinner. It was a lovely, sprawling place, well manicured and very well guarded. We had cocktails outside on the terrace with the other guests, many of them political figures of one kind or another, and then went in for dinner, where we talked about issues facing Rwanda and the Congo. The evening might not have felt much different from others I have experienced—until the president's children came in to find Ben and say hi.

"Could you play basketball with us later?" one of them asked.

"Sure!" Ben said.

I later discovered that on an earlier visit, he had met the four children in the family and spent an afternoon shooting hoops with the boys. Ben had a great ability to connect with people on different levels, mixing seriousness and fun in his approach, and his warmth in developing personal relationships could only help his philanthropic efforts.

We also shared a philosophy in how we approached working as outsiders in the country. Both of us traveled lean and mean, without big entourages or any desire for publicity. Until the campaign, I had always been able to fly under the radar wherever I went, but being with Ben was a whole different experience. Even visiting the grittiest and most unlikely places, he would suddenly be surrounded by young fans. He traveled with a small security team, well needed given his international fame, but he remained pragmatic and hardworking. I've always objected to the parachutists—the celebrities who fly into a poor or troubled country, take a few pictures for social media, and quickly leave again. Ben was the opposite of that. He wanted to learn about the political machinations and find out what mattered to the locals. He was in Africa to make a real difference, not to polish his own résumé.

Some things had changed since my first visit to the Congo, but hunger, corruption, and upheaval were still the norm. There were a lot of internally displaced people (IDP)—those who've had to leave their homes because of regional violence, armed conflict, or humanitarian abuses. They are people just like all of us, caught by circumstances beyond their control. Without means to flee the country, they gather in camps where hunger and disease run rampant.

A few days into the weeklong trip, I went with Ben to tour one of the IDP camps. I had visited many over the years, but for Ben, who was still in his thirties, this was all new. I watched him closely and realized how powerful the experience was for him. He was moved by the unbearable conditions, and I could see that he had the same feeling I did the first time I visited a camp. *It's overwhelming, but I can't abandon these people.* Watching him was both fascinating and educational for me. He wasn't going to be Batman, flying in to save the day (though we did talk about his role in that movie on one trip). Rather, he took it all in so he could figure out the best practical approaches to helping.

On this trip, the plight of women became particularly clear to me. In the eastern Congo, rape is used as a tool of war. The level of violence against women is appalling, terrifying, and insane. Going about your daily life involves a level of risk that is almost hard to fathom. A simple walk into the forest to gather firewood, or down to the stream to draw water, comes with the terror that you could be beaten and raped along the way.

One day, I attended a meeting of Congolese women who had gathered to discuss the rape issue. A successful, educated female lawyer in the region led the conversation. At one point I asked, "How many of you in this room have been raped?" A large portion of the group, including the lawyer, raised their hands.

"You know, it's been three or four months since I've been raped. I'm probably due again," she said. The lawyer wasn't saying it in fear or anger, but as a simple fact of life.

When I heard her say that, I felt a surge of rage and my whole body tensed. No woman should have to live with rape as a way of life.

We're going to stop this, I thought. *We're not going to allow it.* As women of the world, we had to unite and refuse to let women be treated this way.

But my outrage was also mixed with admiration. Whatever challenges they face and however egregiously they are mistreated, African women are very strong. When they manage to gain power and take some control, their communities fare much better. For example, food riots, like the one I witnessed on that earlier trip, still broke out regularly, making it hard to get aid to those who needed it. But more and more now, women had started interceding before the riots began. *This is not going to happen anymore*, they announced. These women worked with the aid organizations to ensure that they would pick up the food and control the flow. When that happened, the food arrived where it was needed. It got to children. It fed families. It was distributed in fair and reasonable fashion.

As I flew home from that trip, I realized that I didn't want to help women because they were vulnerable. I wanted to help them be the ones to change, save, and improve their country.

CHAPTER 11

—⁂—

The Strength of Forgiveness

My trip to the Congo had started me thinking about the power of women to make a change in the region—and my own ability to contribute to that goal. I had no doubt that women could change the balance of power and end some of the rampant corruption. The men in government seemed to know that, too—but since it wasn't in their interest, they continued to do everything they could to hold women down.

One form of suppression occurred at election time. In 2012, I returned to the Congo to observe the second presidential election that kept Joseph Kabila in power. So much was done wrongly and unfairly, and I was particularly incensed at how women were treated.

When you vote in the Congo, you get purple ink on your thumb. People walk around proudly displaying their purple "thumbs up." But women were regularly denied the chance. They would walk together in large groups from their villages to the polling station (there are almost no cars), but when they arrived, the men would tell them "You're at the wrong place. Go five miles in that direction." Of course, there was nothing in that direction. Or if they did get to another polling station, they would be rejected and sent back. It was an abomination. Men found endless ways to torment the women and keep them out of the process.

As an observer, you're not allowed to interfere—all you can do is point out what's wrong and talk about the inadequacies of the system to anyone in or out of the country who will listen. But I had been exasperated on that election day from the start. Around six that morning, I arrived at a polling station outside Goma. Nobody had voted yet—but the ballot boxes were already full.

"What are you going to use when everyone starts voting at eight A.M.?" I asked.

The man overseeing the precinct shrugged. "I think we have some paper boxes out back," he said.

The corruption is infuriating because Africa's potential is so enormous. The people are beautiful and strong, but it happens again and again that they are served poorly by their leaders. Even those who come in promising good intentions often fall into unprincipled behavior and leave their countries worse off.

At the end of that day, I sat down with a group of women who had been sent to three different precincts and never allowed to vote. They were tired and frustrated. Talking to them, it occurred to me that many of the good things I'd seen around Africa had been because women got involved. They needed a place in the system, a way to avoid being trampled and ignored. I started to wonder, could we train women like these to be political candidates themselves? I'd had many years of experience in electoral politics. I could use that to help women get the power—or at least the basic rights—they deserved. Rwanda was one of the great examples of what could happen. As president, Kagame had put more women in leadership roles, and the country's new constitution reserved 30 percent of parliamentary seats for women. Attitudes in-country changed dramatically. In the 2003 election, 48 percent of the seats went to women, and in the next one, women won 64 percent of the seats.

Working with others in the region, I launched a long-term project to get women involved in the politics of other African nations. I was also inspired by the example of Ellen Johnson Sirleaf, who in 2006 became president of Liberia and the first woman to head an African nation. Sirleaf was president of Liberia until 2018 and shared the 2011 Nobel Peace Prize for her efforts to support women's rights and bring women into peacekeeping efforts. I had met her once in Liberia and briefly another time in Washington. She had shown fearlessness in speaking up for fair elections despite the government leaders who tried to silence and imprison her—and her tenacity paid off. Given the conditions in the Congo, I would have been happy with more modest victories than she had achieved. But she had at least shown the world that women leaders in Africa could be both powerful and a source of positive change.

I started gathering information about women in the region who would be good candidates to run for office. The plan was to help them understand all the strategic points that it takes to run a campaign and to give them a leg up in support and fundraising. We weren't encouraging any particular party or position. We just wanted women to understand the fundamentals that would allow them to be part of the process. It was a several-year program, and we educated a couple of dozen women about how to take leadership roles. Empowering women is one of the best ways to make change in a country, and I went back to the Congo regularly to be part of it. But then the violence in the region knocked back our efforts. The Congolese government began threatening, intimidating, and arresting the women surging to be heard. Some of the women we identified and tried to help were threatened with death. For their safety, we stepped back— but I am waiting for the moment when it is safe enough to return and resume our efforts.

I suppose there is some irony in Americans wanting to see more women in leadership roles in Africa, since we've never had a woman president in our own country. The United States is behind much of the world on that score. Women have been the leaders of more than seventy countries, including the United Kingdom, Germany, Norway, Ireland, Finland, Iceland, Denmark, New Zealand, Australia, Pakistan, India, Brazil, Chile, Argentina, Taiwan . . . the list goes on, covering every continent. Americans claim to believe in gender equality. Sadly, we have never been willing to vote for it.

When I heard about the continued atrocities against women in the Congo, I wanted the United States to get involved. I begged my friend Senator Lindsey Graham to come with me on a trip to Africa and see what was going on. It's fine to care about local problems, but in our interconnected world, America needs to be involved in more global concerns. I had heard reports that some UN peacekeeping troops had played a role in violently abusing women. Others suggested that if the UN soldiers weren't perpetrators themselves, they had encouraged the Congolese and not stopped the rape and violence. Either way, it was a tragic situation.

"We need an official delegation," I told Lindsey. "The U.S. needs to take an interest in this."

"I agree," he said. "Let me organize it."

At the time, Lindsey was in control of the U.S. budget for Africa. He pulled together a small delegation of senators for a trip to two or three countries, including Rwanda. We would stay there for a couple of nights and then cross over the border to the Congo. Amazingly, no congressional delegation had ever been to the country before.

Lindsey gathered several senior members of the Senate for the trip, and we flew over in a 737. I was grateful to join the official delegation, but as always when I traveled, I paid for my own expenses and for the seat on the government plane. When the State Department heard about the trip, they were okay with a visit to Rwanda, but they opposed the plan to cross over the border into the Congo. They gave Lindsey a lot of heat. It was too dangerous, they said. They couldn't authorize his going.

"Well, we're going anyway," he told them. "If we don't have an escort into the Congo, I'll drive myself."

The officials gave in—but not before one of them came back with another restriction.

"Mrs. McCain can't go with you," the official said.

"What do you mean?" Lindsey said. "Of course she's coming. She's the reason we're here."

"We can't take responsibility for Cindy McCain crossing the border. Please make sure she's not in the car with you."

Lindsey told me about the conversation, and instead of getting furious at the blatant sexism, I just laughed. I was the only one in our group who had been there before and knew the region—and my need for security was no different from the male senators'. "Fine," I said. "Tell them not to worry. I'll walk."

"You're coming," Lindsey said. "Get in the car."

I brought the senators into the Congo, and we met with some of the key people at the UN outpost. The senators heard different positions, and I let them judge for themselves. When we got back to the United States, there was a congressional investigation. Not long after, the UN officer in charge of the outpost in the Congo was replaced. I don't know that it solved the problems. But it always helps when the people in charge realize that someone is paying attention.

I like being of help in eastern Africa, but I've also learned so much from the perspective and experiences of the people I've met. When I visited the Congo during the 2008 campaign, I met an extraordinary woman who changed how I thought about life's possibilities. She revived my belief in the power of people to be good.

On that visit, I had been invited to witness a conversation between a survivor of the 1990s Rwandan genocide and one of the perpetrators. They were sitting on the same stage, in the same place, talking calmly. The survivor was a woman named Aloisea Inyumba, whose father, a Tutsi, had been killed in the massacre. The perpetrator was the Hutu man who had killed him.

Inyumba had grown up and been educated in Uganda, where her mother had fled with her six children. After college, Inyumba joined a liberation group in Uganda called the Rwandan Patriotic Front. The RPF eventually moved on and achieved its main goal—taking control of Rwanda through a military victory. Many refugees were finally able to return to Rwanda, and Inyumba was one of them. Appointed to the transitional government by Paul Kagame, she soon became a senator and played a key role for the next decade or more in transforming the country and bringing women into important positions. With her efforts, more than half the elected legislators in Rwanda were women—the largest percentage in the world.

All that would have been enough to make me admire her. But as I watched her on that stage, I was truly awed by something in her heart that went far beyond politics. She listened carefully to the man who had killed her father and been a perpetrator of mass genocide—and she forgave him.

Forgave him.

She explained that she was doing this not just for herself, but on behalf of the nation.

After all the horrors she had suffered and the havoc wreaked on her country, anyone would have understood if she wanted retribution. Other people might have demanded justice or vengeance. Instead, she explained on that stage that forgiveness and understanding were the best possible way forward. This was not the first time she had participated in a discussion of reconciliation. The country had made a remarkable turnaround since the genocide, and a large part of it came from the forums she had encouraged on forgiveness. Once again, I realized how women in politics could be a powerful force for good.

I was overwhelmed. Forgiveness doesn't come naturally to most of us—including me. It's easy to hold grudges and hard to let go of them. If someone hurt me or a family member, my first instinct would be anger. Given the chance to confront the person, I would want to lash out and try to make them see that what they had done was indefensible. But if some part of Inyumba felt that way, she had managed to overcome the emotion and redirect it. Instead of anger for the past, she focused on what was required to have hope for the future.

After the event, I got the chance to meet Inyumba. The senator was warm and gracious and didn't think that what she had done was so amazing. We talked about her life and career and her incredible choice of forgiveness. She told me she had chosen to participate in the conversation with the perpetrator for a simple reason.

"It's time to move on for me and my country," she said.

Her goal was to work with everyone and bring rivals to the same table—and I suppose in that way, she reminded me of John. I meet many people when I travel, and I don't always expect to see them again. But as I left that day, I knew that I wanted to stay in touch with Inyumba. I handed her my cellphone and asked her to put in her contact information.

"With pleasure," she said with a broad smile. She told me that since her African name was hard to say, she often went by Ernestine for international meetings.

"Then I'll call you that," I said.

The two of us spoke many times after that. Each time, I felt inspired by her strength and positivity. She wasn't just a political icon—she was a real person with a husband and two children, and we often talked about the pleasures of being a parent. Politics mattered to both of us, but I appreciated that she had balance in her life—caring about home and family, just like I did.

Her inspiration was fresh in my mind when I returned from Africa and got back into the whirlwind of John's 2008 campaign. Talking to her by phone one day, I had an idea. Would she think about coming to America and being my guest at the Republican National Convention? She was someone I wanted people to meet and know about. I was thrilled when she agreed, and we flew her to Minnesota to be in my box at the big event. During my speech, I described her heroism to the crowd, and when a spotlight shone on her, she stood up in the arena and waved.

"Your courage is humbling. Your forgiveness is healing. You are my hero," I said.

She blew me a kiss, and I wanted to run through the crowd and give her a hug. I loved and admired who she was and all she had done.

I thought about Inyumba often after the election and tried to adopt her attitude of forgiveness. Most of us tend to be all about our own little worlds. Someone says an unkind word about us or our spouse, and we decide we dislike them forever. Sometimes we *hate* them. We use that word way too often. I could get furious during campaigns when someone turned nasty about John or tried to hurt him politically. But then you watch people in Rwanda decide to forgive, and it puts so much into perspective. Some of the irritants that fill us with hate shouldn't even be on our radar.

We all know the importance of being a good human being. We say it. We understand what we need to be doing, but too often we get caught up in the moment, and the greater good drifts away. Inyumba helped me realize that "hate" was a word I never wanted to use again. But my conviction about that was tested after John died, when Donald Trump displayed such utter cruelty toward John and my family. The easiest thing for me would be to say *I hate this guy*. His behavior was vile, mean, and childish. But it takes a lot of effort to hate—and you are much better off if you expend effort on good and hopeful things.

John learned that lesson way earlier than most of us. After his years as a POW, he knew that the only way to move on was to forgive his captors. *Let's no longer hate each other.* Even early in our marriage when the experiences were still fresh, he would talk about forgiveness. He never suggested that what the Vietnamese did was right, but he also didn't want to dwell on the past. "There comes a time to heal and stop hating and start having a relationship again," he said.

Normalizing relations with Vietnam was important to John, and he worked hard to make that happen. He visited the country often, meeting the people and the politicians, returning to his prison cell to show that he was no longer angry. Eventually, he stood up against many members of his own party, including Bob Dole and Phil Gramm, in saying that it was time to end the embargo against Vietnam and resume full diplomatic relations. In 1995, he and Senator John Kerry met with President Bill Clinton in the Oval Office to say that the time was right (in fact, well overdue) for normalization. John's closing comment was widely reported.

"It doesn't matter to me anymore, Mr. President, who was for the war and who was against the war," he said. "I'm tired of looking back in anger. What's important is that we move forward now."

John's close working relationship with Kerry was in itself a grand gesture of forgiveness. Kerry had also been a Navy officer during the Vietnam War, but when he returned home, he led a protest against the war. Hundreds of veterans gathered on the Mall in Washington and threw back the medals and ribbons they had won. John heard about the protest from his cell in Hoa Loa prison in Hanoi. Like other prisoners, he felt betrayed. In 1984, when Kerry ran for his first Senate term from Massachusetts, John went to Boston to campaign for Kerry's opponent.

Yet, when both John and Kerry became senators, I watched in

admiration as the two of them overcame their differences. They didn't use the word "forgiveness" at the time, but it's surely what happened. They talked about their wartime experiences and what each had undergone. They listened to each other's stories and points of view. John forgave Kerry for the protests. Kerry forgave John for campaigning against him. They worked together on a Senate select committee to investigate whether any Americans were still in captivity in Vietnam, and they defended and supported each other against people who seemed less interested in the truth than in claiming—without any factual basis—that many Americans remained. John's goal was to bring closure to both sides—and finally end the culture war.

When we took family trips to Vietnam, I understood the power of moving forward. It's a lesson we all need. If John McCain could forgive the Vietnamese, surely his country could, too. If Senator Inyumba could forgive the Hutu man who killed her father, surely the Rwandans could find a way to reconcile. Forgiveness is a gift you give to the other person—but even more to yourself. It frees you from the old grievances and affronts that you can never change.

Political life has become an increasingly angry and divided battlefield, and I often wish we had John's reasoned voice to smooth some of the toxicity. After the 2016 election, we all suffered from the president's endless invective. Whenever I heard the harshness and cruelty Trump regularly spewed, I wondered—how much energy does it take to hate the way you do? Aren't there better ways to spend your time? Trump flounders in a fog of bitterness and pettiness, raging on Twitter about anyone who challenges him or reports accurately on his endless misdeeds. John forgave and lived in a state of optimism. I know which person I would rather be—and which approach is better for our country. I don't like the things Trump said about my husband or the damage he did to America's reputation. But I forgive him. We've got to move on.

Senator Inyumba died of cancer in 2012. Rwandan president

Paul Kagame, who had been her friend for many years, gave the eulogy at her funeral, describing her as a fearless leader whose values would live long after her. She was still in her late forties, so there was much more she could have accomplished. But I prefer to think about all she did achieve in her lifetime—her powerful belief in forgiveness and her equally powerful stance when it came to advancing women. I still have her name and contact number in my cellphone. I won't delete it. I feel comforted each time I look at it and think of her.

In politics, you're always reapplying for your job. Just a couple of weeks after Barack Obama won the 2008 presidential race, John announced that he would seek reelection to his Senate seat in 2010. If he won, it would be his fifth term. At the time, I was exhausted from the just-ended presidential bid and I couldn't imagine starting the cycle all over. I understood that John wanted to do it, and I knew it was the right decision. But it seemed to be happening before we had a moment to catch our breath.

I wanted to be the strong, supportive partner that I usually was during his campaigns—but honestly, I just didn't have it in my gut to give my all again. After you've been knocked down, you're supposed to get right back up and start fighting. John could do that, and eventually I would, too. But I was still feeling a little bruised, and my tender spots needed time to heal. I never actually said aloud to John or myself that I wasn't quite ready to throw myself back into another campaign. But as comics often ask when making a joke about a touchy subject—"Too soon?" For me, 2010 was too soon.

I hung back, but John couldn't. The talk about who would challenge John in 2010 had started almost immediately. We heard that Janet Napolitano, then the popular governor of Arizona, might run on the Democratic line, but then Obama appointed her to the important post of secretary of homeland security. (She later went on to be president of the vast University of California system.) Arizona was generally a solid Republican state, so the biggest hurdle could be in the primary, where the far right wing was revving up. They were prepared to attack John for his bipartisanship and his willingness to help Americans after the 2008 economic crash with an economic stimulus package. John was smart enough to understand every possible angle that an opponent could use, but I'd learned never to say anything like, "Relax, you'll win this." He preferred to run every race like he was coming from behind.

As John pushed ahead, making his case with Arizona voters, I stayed away from the day-to-day grind of campaigning. For the first time ever, I didn't cover events for him, and I stepped way back. John was disappointed not to have me available—but I promised I was rooting from afar. He still won the primary and easily kept his seat in the general election.

"I'm not going to run again," he told me after the votes were in. "That was my last campaign."

"I wouldn't bet on it," I said.

John did run again in 2016, and he won his sixth term. But after that 2010 campaign, we started preparing for what John would do after he left politics. At any stage of life, thinking about what's next can be a good idea. You can enjoy where you are but feel comfortable knowing that when the next stage comes, you'll be ready. I lacked that safety net after the 2008 presidential campaign, and now I understood how important it was. I hadn't floundered for long—but if you have a plan, you can avoid that uncertainty altogether. I think it's particularly important for men and women who have worked in one career most of their lives. If you've been a teacher, doctor, small-business owner, or stay-at-home mom, part of your self-definition is wrapped up in that endeavor. When it ends, the people who do the best have a goal for the next part of their life. It might be playing golf, teaching, spending time with the grandchildren, or volunteering. It needs to be something that gives you a purpose every day. You don't want to leave your career and step into a void.

John talked about creating an institute that would further the goals he always cared about. Our friend Bob Dole, the longtime senator from Kansas, had set up the Dole Institute of Politics at the University of Kansas a few years earlier. Dole had been the Republican nominee for president in 1996 (losing to Bill Clinton) and for vice president in 1976 (when he and Gerald Ford lost to Jimmy Carter and Walter Mondale). Ronald Reagan also had an institute to further the principles he championed, global democracy and liberty. John liked the idea of using them as models. We could create the McCain Institute to give John a place to carry on his work. But what would it look like?

We spent a lot of long evenings talking about the issues we each found compelling. John kept coming back to the basic freedoms that America represents around the world. When you talk about the rule of law or freedom of the press, it can sound distant and theoretical—but those issues have a profound effect on how we live every day. Millions of people around the world lack those basic freedoms, and in recent years, Americans have seen how easily they could slip away from us, too.

John would get outraged whenever he heard about a reporter in another country being arrested or killed. Attacking the press is a common ploy of autocrats and dictators who want to hide the truth. They oppose an open press that holds them accountable—and you know a country is in trouble when its leader tries to challenge and undermine press freedoms. Similar problems arise when leaders bend laws to maintain their own power.

As John and I talked, we realized that so much came down to encouraging character-driven leadership. He imagined creating a global network of leaders who believed in ethics and values, and who conducted themselves in ways that commanded respect. Barely a decade later, I see how prescient John was in his belief that a corrupt, self-involved leader can create havoc even in the strongest of countries. He wanted to develop a generation of young leaders with strong character around the world, a cause that seems more pressing than ever.

As we laid out plans, John turned the question to me. "We need to have room at the institute for your passions, too," he said.

"Will we have his and her sides?" I asked, teasing.

"All for one and one for all," he said.

The humanitarian causes that interested me—including human trafficking, human rights, and women's issues—became a part of the institute from the start. It was a place where I could continue my efforts with the Congo and work all over Africa to encourage women's leadership. I was excited to have a team to work with and a structure to hold together these many different projects.

We launched the McCain Institute in 2012 with Arizona State University. The connection with the university was perfect in extending our reach. We had headquarters in Washington, D.C., and a number of programs based in Arizona. In some ways, it was the institute version of the life John and I had always had—making things happen in D.C. and Phoenix and letting each piece enhance the other. We worked with ASU to educate students on political values, offering a master's program in international affairs and a program to teach law students about the rule of law and good governance in countries riddled by conflict. We created leadership programs and partnered with governments to combat terrorism and improve global security. We launched the Sedona Forum, an annual gathering of leaders and activists to come up with real-world solutions to pressing problems. And that was just the start. Our offerings were both broad and deep. It drove John crazy when anyone referred to the McCain Institute as a "think tank." Maybe it doesn't sound as fancy, but we always saw it as a Do Things kind of place.

John and I delighted in getting the institute started and watching the staff begin their work. We didn't know then that John would never get to work on it full-time. The Senate, it turned out, would be his final workplace.

CHAPTER 12

Something Is Wrong

Many people were feeling a little skittish after the 2016 presidential election, so I didn't get worried at first when John seemed to have less energy than usual. The election had turned everything upside down. The boorish, self-focused candidate whom most Republicans considered vastly unqualified for the job won the party's nomination. John endorsed him out of loyalty, even after Trump made shockingly rude remarks about John's military career. But shortly before the election, when the *Access Hollywood* tape came out with Trump describing how he likes to grab women "by the pussy," John had had enough. He was repulsed by what he heard and withdrew the endorsement. He couldn't vote for a man who bragged about sexual assault.

John and I talked about the tape, but I didn't have to convince him of anything. We both found it abhorrent. Years earlier, we had talked about how the dynamics of professional relationships had changed. "You've got to make sure women feel equal in your office," I told him often, and he had followed that advice. When talking with the young men and women on his staff, he listened to everyone and made sure that all points of view were in the mix. We both believed that America had taken big strides in equality for women, so it was understandable that after the tape went public, Billy Bush, the TV host who Trump had been boasting to on the tape, lost his job on the *Today* show—but almost unfathomable that Trump went on to become president.

The night of the election, we had a party at the Heard Museum in Phoenix to celebrate John's sixth Senate victory. He had been leading by double digits in the polls, but he never took his own reelection for granted. For the top of the ticket, though, we thought Hillary Clinton had victory in the bag. When it became clear sometime around midnight that Trump would win the electoral college, we were shocked. He lost the popular vote by some three million votes, so it's fair to say that a majority of the country was also shocked and unhappy.

"I don't recognize what's happening in the country, but it's my job to help him be a good president," John said when we finally went to sleep.

I was glad that John had won, but I worried about where America might be headed. Everything many of us believed about the values of the Republican Party seemed to be shaken.

I thought ruefully of the work I'd done around the world to promote women's issues and halt sexual exploitation. Maybe I needed to focus my efforts on our country now.

Sometime after the election, I started to sense John wasn't himself. He snapped at people and he was harsh sometimes—which wasn't like him. John had long been pegged as a guy with a temper, but in more than thirty years of marriage he had never once lost his temper with me. Never once. Our marriage didn't work that way, and I think he knew I wouldn't have tolerated it. Now he was edgy with me and everyone else in a way I didn't recognize. When I pointed out that he was acting differently, he pointed to all the disruptions in the party and in Washington.

"Chalk it up to fatigue," he said. "I'm just overworked."

"You always work hard," I said gently.

"Well, then, I apologize if I've been difficult."

"You haven't done anything wrong. I'm just worried about you," I said.

For as long as I'd known him, John was an up-and-ready guy. Six hours of sleep, and he would be raring to go, zipping around the world without any signs of weakness. Now he slept for twelve hours a day, and he still seemed logy. When the kids were home, they, too, noticed something was different. None of us could quite put a finger on what was wrong. We all talked about it, and one day, Meghan brought it up to John.

"It's my age catching up with me," he told her. "I'm eighty years old."

"You don't think anything else is wrong?" she asked.

He shook his head and gave her a reassuring hug.

John had never acted his age before—he had remained energetic and vibrant even as the years passed. Younger colleagues often sighed that they could barely keep up with him. If people on his staff noticed a change, they didn't say anything. But then the staff as well as the whole country *had* to notice—and all of us were stunned to see a John McCain we didn't recognize, live and on television.

It happened in early June when former FBI chief James Comey was called to testify before the Senate Intelligence Committee. The media was out in force for the questioning, which focused on Russia's interference in the 2016 election and their possible collusion with the Trump campaign. After more than two and a half hours with Comey on the stand, John was the last senator to question him. Maybe he was tired. He had certainly lost concentration. John asked one question and then another. He mumbled and got confused. He referred to the president as "Comey," and he seemed to conflate the FBI investigation into the Hillary Clinton emails with the Russian investigation. It was completely unlike John McCain.

I watched the hearing live from our home in Phoenix. I never made a habit of tuning in for John's political moments, but I was interested in this one. When I heard him talking, a cold chill ran through me. I was stunned. John was always so well prepared. He had a steel-trap memory and a steel-trap mind, but now he had gotten himself muddled making an equivalency between the Hillary Clinton investigation—which had concluded by then—and the one still ongoing into the president's behavior. I knew that Lindsey Graham, who wasn't on the committee, had texted a question to John, and I wondered if that had been the problem. Maybe Lindsey's question hadn't made sense to him, and he was trying to improvise around it?

My gut told me that wasn't the case. John was usually smart enough on these issues that if something wasn't clear to him, he could wing it and still sound more knowledgeable than most other politicians. For him to get confused this way didn't make sense. After the televised hearings, some commentators thought that John had gotten into a tangle trying to defend Trump. But John had been reasonably critical of the president in the past. Why would he twist himself into knots trying to defend him now?

After the hearing, his staff told him that people were worried about his confused appearance. *The Washington Post* had headlined his "bizarre" questioning of Comey and described one of the exchanges as "weird." John was mortified. He couldn't explain what had happened, but he managed to respond with his usual brand of humor. "Maybe going forward I shouldn't stay up late watching the Diamondbacks night games," he said in a statement, referring to the Arizona baseball team. He went on to clarify that he was trying to ask

Mr. Comey whether the president's actions constituted obstruction of justice. If he hadn't stated it properly in the hearing, he would submit it in writing for the record.

It was a good political save. But the person at that hearing was not the John McCain I knew. Maybe it was a blip and he really was just working too hard. I wanted him to come home for the upcoming Senate recess and relax at our cabin; he could wander through our property, enjoy the birds and trees and wildlife, take part in the Fourth of July parties we used to have with friends and games and spirited outdoor dinners. For the past dozen or so years, ever since the Iraq War, John had spent every Fourth visiting American forces in Afghanistan and Iraq. He was always moved by the reenlistment ceremonies that took place on that day, where soldiers signed up for another tour of duty. He celebrated America's independence by honoring the people fighting for it.

John brought a few Senate colleagues along with him on this trip, including a couple of old friends and two first-term senators—the very conservative David Perdue of Georgia and the very liberal Elizabeth Warren of Massachusetts. He always took delight in bringing together people who might not normally spend long periods of time with each other. It was his private attempt at encouraging collegiality and friendly understanding among his colleagues. Everything about the trip went well, but he came back exhausted.

"I never used to get jet lag, but this trip wiped me out," he told me.

It was becoming a pattern. Just before the Comey hearing, John had taken another trip—to Australia and Vietnam—and come home tired, saying that the staff had pushed him too hard. I'd never ever heard him complain about that before.

"What did they do wrong?" I asked him.

"I was exhausted. They just pushed me and pushed me. The trip was bad. That's why I don't feel good and made that gaffe at the hearing."

Even so, he wasn't slowing down. He went back to Washington, and I went to our place in Coronado, California, where I loved to be in the summer, in part to escape the Arizona heat. John had his annual physical scheduled for a week or so later at the Mayo Clinic in Phoenix. He was flying back for it, and I told him that I wanted to join him this time.

"Nothing is going to be wrong, so there's no reason to come back," John said.

"I'm happy to be there," I said.

"Really, it's nothing. I'll be in and out of here in no time. Stay where you are and enjoy the ocean."

However concerned I felt, I knew John wouldn't be happy if I fussed about his health, so I agreed to stay where I was. He went for his checkup on a Friday. He told his doctors about his excessive fatigue and the confusion at the Comey hearing, and they ran some additional tests, including a brain scan. John left the clinic that afternoon, sure that all was well. He was heading up to the cabin to spend the night there when he got a call from his doctor.

"Please turn around immediately and come back," she said.

"It's Friday afternoon," John said. "Why don't I come in on Monday?"

"No, this is urgent. Please turn around."

John turned around. On the way back to Phoenix, he called the director of his state office, a lovely young woman named Michelle Shipley, and asked her to meet him at the hospital. John's longtime friend and former campaign manager Rick Davis was in town, and he arrived, too. Rick reached me in Coronado to say that I needed to get right home.

"Have they said what's wrong?" I asked.

"Not yet, but it's serious," Rick said.

"I'm glad you're there. I'll hop on the first plane and be there very soon."

Getting back to Phoenix wasn't as easy as usual. It was summertime and the flights from Coronado were all full. I finally managed to get a seat on a plane, and landing in Phoenix, I rushed over to the Mayo Clinic. By that point, John was already in surgery. I was stunned by the urgency, and I realized something must be seriously wrong if the doctors decided to operate a few hours after seeing the scan.

A friend once compared waiting while a loved one is in surgery to waiting for the verdict after a trial. When the jury (or surgeon) comes back, you wait breathlessly to see if they smile at you. If they smile, you're fine. If there's no expression, you're doomed.

When the surgeons finally came out of the operating room and sat down to talk to me, I didn't see a lot of smiles. They told me they had removed a two-inch blood clot from above John's left eye. They cut into his skull to reach the clot, but only had to make a small incision above his eyebrow. It was a minimally invasive procedure.

That was the good news.

The pathology reports would take a few days, and the doctors would need the lab findings to confirm what they had seen. However, they wanted to be completely straightforward with me. They believed the clot had been caused by a brain cancer. Possibly glioblastoma, the most aggressive form of the disease.

Those were the words they used, but they didn't make any sense to me. John had faced a couple of bouts with melanoma over the years, but they were always the least dangerous kind and easily handled. But brain cancer? Glioblastoma? I was in disbelief. The doctors went on to explain that there were several different types of brain cancer and the pathology would tell us more.

I already knew more than I wanted to. I was reeling, but I pulled myself together and walked into John's recovery room. Just out of surgery, he was already sitting up, alert and talking to people. How could this be? The doctors just told me he likely had a brain tumor. But look at him! He was the regular John McCain, an amazing human being with superhuman strength, carrying on conversations and holding court. I couldn't get any of it to make sense. It all felt surreal, like I was floating in some space between dreamworld and netherworld.

John came home the next day, a little glazy from the surgery but stronger than anyone would have expected. His office issued a statement about the blood clot and explained it had been removed by a "minimally invasive craniotomy." Senator McCain would be home recovering for a week. The press jumped on the story, but doctors at the Mayo Clinic wouldn't give any interviews. They told us that it would be inappropriate to say anything more until the pathology reports came back. The hospital promised to release more information when it became available. By Sunday, several newspapers were speculating about what the clot could mean and what had caused it. *The New York Times* let various doctors opine about subdural hematomas and blood thinners and various other topics that had nothing at all to do with the truth.

On Tuesday, when John's stitches were due to come out, three doctors from the Mayo Clinic came to our house—the neurosurgeon, an assistant surgeon who actually took out the stitches, and John's personal physician. When I saw that all of them had come, I knew it wasn't going to be good. They proceeded to tell us what was wrong, and there was no way to sugarcoat it. The lab confirmed what the doctors had expected—John had a primary glioblastoma. "Primary" meant the cancer had started there and not spread from anywhere else. The surgeon had removed all of it, but cells are almost always left behind, which meant the cancer would come back. John was in good shape and recovering quickly from the surgery, and they said that was positive. But then the doctors mentioned that glioblastoma was the same cancer that had taken Senator Ted Kennedy's life.

Suddenly, the severity of the diagnosis became all the more real. We could put a face on it. Ted and John had been great colleagues

and friends. Despite coming from different political parties and ide-
ologies, they had joined together on major issues like healthcare.
John often said that he and Ted could make fervent speeches opposing each other on the floor of the Senate—then pat each other on the
back and walk out as friends. Now they were bound by a terrible
diagnosis.

In another tragic coincidence, John's longtime friend Joe Biden
had lost his son Beau to glioblastoma two years earlier. As with Ted
Kennedy, John differed on many political issues with Biden, but they
were fiercely loyal and admiring of each other. Joe once described
them as brothers from different fathers. Even before John, this terrible disease had come too close to us.

The facts about glioblastoma don't provide much comfort. It is a
particularly brutal form of cancer, and the survival rate—even for one
year—is extremely low. The standard treatment included radiation
and chemotherapy. As the doctors sat in our house, discussing the
pathology and next steps, John listened carefully. Then he looked
intently at the doctors and said, "Tell me the straight story. I can take
it." He wanted to know what to expect and how much time he had.
They wouldn't answer him directly, explaining that every case has
many variables.

"Don't dodge around," John said sharply. "I want to know what's
what so we can make a plan."

Despite the circumstances, I gave a little smile. John always liked
to have a plan. But the doctors continued to hedge. People responded
differently to medication and treatment, they said, and they couldn't
predict any individual outcome.

Given all that John and I had each been through in our lives, we
basically believed we could get through anything. We weren't trying to hide anything, so we shared the story with Dr. Sanjay Gupta
and asked him to break the news. John had great respect for Gupta;
as the chief medical correspondent on CNN, he would set the right

tone. Gupta asked for permission to speak to John's doctors, and we said sure. All we wanted was for the news to be correct. Some staff members were with us at our house when the report came on, and we all watched it together in silence. Gupta reported accurately. Having the world know the story made it all the more painfully real.

The news spread fast from there, and we started getting supportive comments on Twitter from politicians around the country and leaders around the world. President Obama wrote, *John McCain is an American hero & one of the bravest fighters I've ever known. Cancer doesn't know what it's up against. Give it hell, John.*

We greatly appreciated the support and the warmth, and the message from Obama was particularly gratifying. The former political foes had become each other's admirers. John had shown unmatched strength and tenacity for his whole life, and he would never quit on himself or anyone else. I was still in disbelief, but I had to agree. Cancer had never met anyone like John before.

When John got his diagnosis, Congress was in the midst of a debate on healthcare—one of the topics that America still hasn't gotten right. Republicans were arguing to repeal and replace Obamacare, and John had run for Senate on that platform. It was going to be a tight vote, and while still home in Phoenix, John had mixed feelings. He wanted the Republicans and Democrats to work together and try to reach some compromise, which he considered the basis for our democracy to continue. He didn't think that the pretense of ideological purity should ever become more important than doing what was best for the people of the country. The Republican bill as it currently stood would repeal Obamacare without replacing it, leaving millions of Americans without any healthcare at all. John had some hope that with his proper urging, the two sides would come together on a true replacement.

Meanwhile, the doctors wanted to start his treatment immediately.

"Great," John said. "We'll do it as soon as I get back from Washington."

Get back? That meant he would be going. We had a bit of a row in the family, with all of us trying to keep John from traveling. He would have to fly across the country, and the doctors were strongly opposed to him doing that so soon after brain surgery. John listened, but as always, he came to his own decision.

"I'm going to do this," he told me. "I'm still here and I'm still kicking, and this is too important not to go."

"The doctors don't want you flying," I reminded him.

"I owe it to the people of Arizona to vote on this issue," he said.

I shook my head. I'd been married to John long enough to know that once he invoked his sense of responsibility to his constituents, to America, or to the brave military men and women fighting for our country, I didn't stand a chance.

We got a private plane, and I flew with John back to Washington. We went directly to the Capitol building, where the debate over repeal was already taking place—and as John walked onto the Senate floor, the entire chamber erupted into prolonged applause. Watching from the gallery, I was completely overcome. I'd been around these members a long time, and I'd never seen anything like the emotion that flowed toward John in that moment. Senators came over to hug him, and people like Bernie Sanders, who didn't agree with John on anything, got too choked up to speak. I saw at least one senator weeping openly as John came over. Then, with all the love swirling his way, John took the floor for his speech.

I watched and listened as he described being in the Senate as "the most important job I've had in my life." Given the military service

John had done earlier, it was a strong statement. Then he went on to scold the senators, saying that while the Senate was meant to be a principled and deliberative body, the increase in partisanship and tribalism threatened its role and they weren't getting much done for the American people. Both sides had contributed to the current decline and needed to remember their bigger goals. Sometimes chipping away at problems didn't feel like a political triumph, but it was part of governing. The senators had to remember that they had a powerful role. "We are not the president's subordinates," John said. "We are his equal!" To preserve that role, they had to come together and do the work they had been elected to do.

When he finished speaking, there was another swell of emotion in the chamber. People lined up to thank him, to wish him well, to offer him their love and prayers. I stood outside and waited for a long time. For a brief moment, my fears about the future were offset by my incredible pride in my husband.

Over the next couple of days, people lobbied for John's vote on the healthcare repeal bill. Republicans assumed he had returned to Washington and delayed his treatments so he could be part of the vote to kill Obamacare for good. But John wanted provisions that would help people who would lose their healthcare if the bill passed. He wasn't trying to preserve Obamacare—he just wanted Congress to come up with a real alternative. He urged a new legislative effort, with input from Republicans and Democrats, to create a healthcare system that was fair and workable.

John listened carefully to both sides and to all possibilities, but he didn't see any progress in the right direction. The night of the vote, nobody was sure which way John would vote. Tension was building, and with almost everyone in the Senate voting along party lines, his was likely to be the deciding vote. When some reporters called out to ask what he planned to do, John shot back: "Wait for the show!"

He wasn't being a show-off. He just wanted to let his colleagues in the Senate know his plan before the press announced it. As the senators swarmed the floor making their last-minute appeals, John let a few key members know his decision. Finally, after midnight, John cast his vote. He said "No" and gave a thumbs-down gesture, signaling his opposition to the bill as it stood to repeal the healthcare law.

I didn't support Obamacare, but I knew that what John had done was both brave and right. He was championing compromise and putting the people of the country over politics. He didn't need a cancer diagnosis to make him follow his convictions. He had done it his whole life.

After the vote, we traveled back to Phoenix together. For once, the wild headlines about John didn't make much of an impact on me. Some hailed him as the hero whose integrity had saved people's healthcare from being ripped away. Others sniped about his being one of three Republicans who had crossed party lines with his vote. John took it in stride. He had never fit into a box. He thought his speech and his vote had made the point. For the Senate to function, it needed problem solvers, not purists.

John had felt comfortable being in Washington at the heart of a national debate, but I was relieved to get him back home where he could begin his cancer treatments. When you get a diagnosis like this, it starts out feeling unreal, like you've tumbled into a life that isn't yours. *I'm the person with the strong, invincible husband, not the wife of the guy who has cancer! There must be some mistake!* Then the reality descends and the onslaught of information comes at you fast, with too much force. All of a sudden, it's as if you're in medical school. You're learning about care and therapies and outcomes and using words that have never been in your vocabulary before. You try to take in as much as you can.

The first round of treatments included oral chemotherapy and proton radiation at the Mayo Clinic, and it really wasn't so bad. We were warned that John would feel very tired afterward, and that indeed happened. But there was no dramatic hair loss or nausea or some of the other side effects that people fear. The biggest problem was actually getting the drugs. John had health insurance through the Senate, which you assume would be pretty good—but I found myself on the phone with the insurance company, arguing for his chemotherapy.

"Do you really think he needs it?" asked the representative on the phone.

"His doctors have ordered it," I said. "How can you even ask that question?"

"I'd like to find an alternative," she said.

I couldn't believe it. Was the insurance company really trying to deny my husband the treatment he needed? We argued back and forth for a few minutes, but I could feel myself getting nowhere. All the debates about health insurance that had been so politically divisive in the past few days—and in the years before that—suddenly landed hard in my lap. They went from theoretical to very personal. Being at the mercy of an insurance company for life-and-death action is terrifying. And not everyone can do what I did next. I realized that the Senate used the same insurance carrier as our family business, though ours was a more premium plan, and I decided to pull out all the stops.

"Look, my name is Cindy McCain," I said. "In addition to being John McCain's wife, I own the Hensley company. I have sixteen hundred employees, and you are our healthcare provider. If you want me to pull the plug on those policies now, I will. You can explain to your bosses why."

"Oh, well, I guess you can have the chemotherapy," she said

grudgingly. "You have to fill it at our pharmacy and you can have it in two weeks."

"No to both of those," I said adamantly. "You will fill it today at the Mayo Clinic pharmacy and I will pick it up in an hour."

When I hung up the phone, every nerve in my body was on edge. It was a little like the day I stood up to the male authorities in Bangladesh to get two infants out of the country. Sometimes my backbone goes up, and I will go through fire to get what's needed and what's right. But as I drove to the pharmacy that day, I was outraged that I'd had to use the power of my company to ensure that my husband got chemotherapy. I thought about the despair other people would feel on that phone conversation and the wild inequities in the system. Yes, John was right about healthcare. For once, Republicans and Democrats had to work together and think about the bigger picture. This was just too important for political games.

Not long after the diagnosis, we got a call from Lesley Stahl, the reporter for CBS's *60 Minutes*. She wanted to do a story about John. We had known her forever and we agreed. She came up to the cabin, and John walked around with her, showing the old-growth trees, the rippling brook, and the beautiful birds. He loved being in nature and seeing the richness and diversity of life.

"It puts everything in perspective," he told her.

Later that day, the two of us sat down with Stahl for an interview. She referred to John as an "indestructible man," which was certainly how I saw him. He had survived everything that war and mortal enemies could throw his way. But now John told her that his cancer was serious and "it's a very poor prognosis." I had known that was the case. But somehow, hearing John say it in public, for the world to understand, shook me deeply. I tried to stay composed and not break into tears—but I was thrown by what John said next. He gave a smile and explained that while he would get good doctors and do the best he could, he also planned to celebrate a life well lived. "Every night when I go to sleep, I'm so filled with gratitude," he said.

Gratitude. It's probably not the first emotion most people have after a cancer diagnosis, but John felt it at his core. Later that night, after Stahl and her large behind-the-camera contingent had left and the grounds were quiet again, I brought up the topic with John. He told me he was grateful that he had been able to serve his country in the Senate for three decades. When he looked back to years of torture and impris- onment in Hanoi, he was grateful for the close friendships he had made with the other POWs. He felt gratitude to me and the children for the love and support and closeness we had shared for so long.

I listened carefully. I had learned so much from John over the years. Maybe I could take this lesson, too.

The grim prognosis had shaken me deeply, and it had also shocked John. But he insisted that he went to bed each night filled with grati- tude. My nights were different—I lay in bed riven by anxiety and disbelief and unable to sleep. Late that night, as I tossed and turned, I decided to focus on all the reasons I had to be grateful. It was easy enough to make a list: the wonderful years with my husband, my fabulous children, the experiences I'd had around the world. As I clicked through my mental inventory, I felt myself relaxing.

Once again, John was right. However dire your situation may be, you can find reasons to be grateful. As I drifted off to sleep, I thought that being filled with positive feelings was a lot better than being overcome with fear and anger.

After starting the first round of treatment that summer, John was deter- mined to go to an international security conference at Lake Como.

Given the new administration, he felt it was more important than ever to have the values he cared about heard by major world leaders.

Everyone in our family agreed on one thing—he shouldn't go. An international flight of long duration at high altitude? I left it to the kids to try talking some sense into him, but their warnings about dangers didn't carry much weight. I ended up accompanying him to the conference—because what else could I do?

That was the trip where I got on the plane with John and told him that I was waiting for his brain to explode. He told me I shouldn't worry—he had a dustbuster to clean up any mess. Over the years, we had learned to laugh together through disagreements. If you're not going to change each other's minds, you're better off making fun of the situation than getting angry.

Lake Como is always a beautiful place to visit, and once we landed (with John's brain still intact), I tried to convince myself that some good Italian food and fresh mountain air would serve John well. But rather than seeking some much-deserved pleasures, John had come with a strong sense of responsibility. He understood international relations better than anyone I knew, and people around the world listened to him. With the Trump administration undermining our alliances and refusing to stand up for basic freedoms, John felt someone needed to speak for America's continued role in the world. And so he did.

In a speech that garnered international attention, John noted that a strong relationship between the United States and our European allies was important for all of our common security. He admitted that there was a debate in the country about what America's role should be with other nations. How that debate played out could determine the future of the world. At a fancy dinner that night, many people told John how valuable his talk had been and thanked him for being there. They appreciated his bluntness and his willingness to admit the change in America that was being whispered about across the globe. Many believed that Trump had little interest in longtime allies and could be dangerously disruptive. John's comments gave them hope that not all American leaders had swung away from pursuing global stability, and that reason might yet prevail.

As we left the dinner, my feelings toward the conference shifted. I was glad that John had done what he'd wanted. His words that day had mattered. If I had to pack the dustbuster on the way home—well, maybe it was worth it.

When the Senate went back into session in the fall, John returned to Washington. He thrived on being there, so I made the decision to drop everything to be with him full-time. He began a second round of treatments at the National Institutes of Health (NIH), which were a little tougher on him—but he still got his treatments in the morning and then showed up on the Senate floor immediately after. At one point, the doctors put him on steroids, which alarmed me as much as anything. I know they can do wonders, but they also have debilitating side effects.

The steroids made John's legs so weak that he fell once in our Washington apartment. I tried to get him up, but I wasn't in condition to win any weight-lifting contests. Back on Memorial Day, I had fallen during a family trip to Disneyland and snapped my humerus, the bone between your shoulder and your elbow. I couldn't believe how badly it hurt. I flew back to Phoenix, where doctors set the bone and put on an external fixator to hold it in place. In pictures of me from that summer of John's diagnosis, you can see straps wrapped around my upper arm on the outside of my clothes, like some bizarre fashion statement gone wrong.

I still had the brace on when John fell in the apartment, and trying to get him off the floor displaced my arm all over again. Once again, I went back to the Mayo Clinic in Phoenix, and this time they had to put a plate inside. I stayed just a couple of days and then flew back to Washington in a sling. I couldn't worry about my weak arm for long because much bigger medical issues were swirling around John.

John continued going to his office and working, but health setbacks started coming at him in a constant barrage. He tried to stay upbeat, but it is unsettling to constantly face hurdles that you can't readily surmount.

One day he lapsed into unconsciousness. Not knowing what was happening, I called an ambulance and got him to NIH. It turned out to be a kind of diabetic coma, which occurs when your blood sugar levels spike or fall dramatically low. John had never had diabetes before; it was yet another side effect of the steroids. After that, he was on insulin three times a day and various other protocols. Then he took a minor misstep in early November and, with his joints weakened from the steroids, ended up in Walter Reed hospital with a torn Achilles tendon. He got a walking boot and went right back to work. For John, being hobbled and slowed was almost as bad as the cancer itself. "I can't tell you how much I hate wearing this boot!" he wrote in a tweet, which included a photo of him with boot and cane. It was easier to joke about a boot than some of the other complications.

Despite getting weaker, John was determined to get to the Army-Navy football game that year. The game was being played in Philadelphia in early December, and we started making arrangements so he could get there comfortably and not have to walk too far when he arrived. Any kind of travel was getting increasingly complicated.

"I'm not sure this is a good idea," I told him.

"It will be my last Army-Navy game. I want to be there," he said.

On the morning of the game, it started to snow. John stared dolefully out the window and listened to the weather reports predicting blizzard conditions in Philly. Finally, about an hour before we were supposed to leave, he gave a sigh. "I don't think we ought to do this," he said.

My relief that he had come to his senses came with a wave of sadness. John still had the drive to do so much, and his mind and heart were as determined as ever. But his physical self would no longer cooperate. However much he loved Washington, we needed to get back home. It was becoming clear to me that I had to have help, and he was soon going to need full-time care. Not long after that, we left Washington and returned to the cabin. Over the years, we had built new homes and structures on the land and nurtured the trees and vegetation. We all felt cosseted here, and I knew John would be secure. I just didn't know how much time we would have to enjoy it.

CHAPTER 13

⋘⋙

Celebrating Life

J oy and sadness mix more easily than most of us realize. The final
year of John's life was shattering for our family, yet we also had
moments of laughter and happiness. One day of sheer jubilation
occurred Thanksgiving week when Meghan got married at our ranch.
The ceremony took place on the lawn, with the creek burbling
behind. John had just torn a second Achilles tendon, so instead of
walking her down the aisle, he waited at the front to give her away.
Meghan is too strong a woman to like the actual meaning of that
phrase, but she was willing to overlook it if it meant having that
moment of tradition with her dad at her wedding.

Meghan's engagement hadn't been a total surprise—she had been
dating Ben Domenech for a while. When John started his radiation
treatments in July at the Mayo Clinic, Meghan insisted on being
right there with him. Ben stayed at her side. The hospital gave us a
little auxiliary room in which to wait, and one day as John came out
of radiation, Meghan and Ben emerged from the room with big

smiles on their faces. In the middle of the corridor, Meghan said, "Ben just asked me to marry him and we're going to get married." John's eyes filled with tears, and I thought, *What? What just happened?* Meghan was terribly distraught about John in those months, but the decision gave us all a moment of hope.

Meghan kept the engagement quiet, but by the end of September, she'd decided that she needed to accelerate all her plans. Nothing was more important than having her dad at her wedding.

"What do you think about our getting married in November at the cabin?" she asked me one day.

I thought for a moment. It would leave us five weeks or so to plan a wedding. "Okay, we can do that," I said.

"I'm thinking about a western hunting lodge theme."

"Well, we're in the West," I said. "If that's what you want, that's what we'll do."

I made it sound easy, but I was truly worried about whether or not I could pull it off. I knew I could handle the abbreviated timing and still arrange for the perfect tents and the right tablecloths. But a wedding is more than a party. You want to be fully there and present for your child, not just going through the motions. At that point, my emotions were fully consumed with John, and I wasn't sure that I could swing from my total focus on his health and future to give Meghan the full-hearted attention she deserved. But I was determined to try.

Weddings can take a long time to plan—or barely a month. Jimmy had gotten married on our property a couple of years earlier, and I'd enjoyed working out the details. He and his wife, Holly, had known each other for ten years before their wedding, and their big day turned out to be spirited and festive and just their style. Now I called an event planner who had worked with us on other parties, and he and Meghan whipped up their plans to turn our calm woods into the Wild West.

On the day of the ceremony, she walked down an aisle covered with cowhides and stood under an arch of birch branches and elk horns. The dinner afterward included lots of wild game, and the party had the vibe of the Old West, with slot machines and poker tables and a great band. The reception was packed with Meghan and Ben's buddies from the media and friends Meghan had made in the 2008 campaign. When the bride and groom went to cut the cake, it was layered so high that it was taller than both of them and cleverly decorated with leaves and antlers. The whole evening, Meghan beamed in joy.

Meghan's joy spread to all of us—and despite my conflicting emotions, I managed to disentangle from the miasma of cancer and feel the pleasure of the day. I realized it was a very good thing for the whole family to come together in happiness.

Instead of going on a honeymoon, Meghan and Ben stayed with us at the cabin, and Ben couldn't have been more understanding when his new wife spent a lot of that time away from him and talking to her dad. We often said that Meghan and John were two sides of the same coin, and we still teased Meghan for being John-in-a-skirt. Now she was losing her dad, friend, adviser, role model, and sparring partner, and she wanted to hold on to him as long as she could.

A few weeks earlier, John had been a guest on *The View*, where Meghan was the newest co-host. John sat next to her and glided easily between wit and warmth. Longtime co-host Joy Behar pointed out that John had a great sense of humor. Could Meghan's soon-to-be husband ever match Dad? When the subject of Meghan's wedding came up, she admitted that after dating a lot of liberals who her dad didn't like, she had ended up "with the most conservative guy in the history of the world." At the end of the segment, John gave her a little gift—a framed photo of her and John hiking in Sedona. Meghan started to cry. "I'm the luckiest person in the world," she said to her dad. "We have such a bond, such a love."

Meghan had come to us for advice when she was first offered the spot on *The View*. It was just after John's diagnosis, and she knew that John and I didn't have great feelings about that show. John and I had appeared on it both individually and together during the 2008 campaign, and the mostly liberal hosts bit at our heels. After our last appearance, we both left saying "We're done." I could understand differences on substantive issues, but what was I supposed to say when Joy Behar declared I wasn't a natural blonde? I suggested she look at my children, or check out my baby pictures, where I was pure towhead from the start. And really, just how natural was that red hair of hers? I should never resort to that level of trifling, but I felt mistreated. The hosts were ruthless.

But when Meghan got the offer, John was happy to cast all that aside.

"I think you should do it," he said. "We've had our differences with them, but this is a great opportunity, and that's what really counts." The show aired nationally, getting huge attention and making a big impact five days a week. It was pure John to be able to get past a personal experience and see this was a great step for Meghan's career.

"As long as you know what you'll be in for as the one conservative host," he said.

"I do. It won't be a surprise," she said.

Then she asked my opinion. I thought about it for a moment. I was the one who held grudges, but I knew John was right. This was a great opportunity and just the right platform for her.

"I think you're well suited for the show," I said. "Like your dad, you can handle anything."

Meghan nodded and John pointed out that with her strong voice and good perspective, the show would be lucky to have her.

"I agree. Go for it," I said. "Just don't ask anyone about their hair color."

For the next months, Meghan spent most of her time in New

York, doing *The View* live every day and coming back to the cabin as often as she could on weekends and days off. I set a timer on my phone so I would tune in every morning and not miss a moment. If someone had told me after 2008 that I would become *The View*'s biggest fan, I wouldn't have believed it—but I smiled at the unexpected twist and the good lesson. You have to be open to everything.

As much as I wanted our children close, I understood the demands of their lives made that tough. Jack was on active duty in the Navy in Afghanistan and couldn't get home much. He was deployed teaching Afghan pilots to fly helicopters. As a Navy helicopter pilot himself, he had been based on an aircraft carrier in the region before, but he was always on a ship and never on the ground. He wanted the challenge of working closely with the Afghanis and helping them succeed on their own. He spoke fluent Farsi, Dari, and some other dialects, so he was a great choice—but the danger of the mission terrified me. His wife, Renee, an officer in the Air Force, was based at Andrews Air Force Base and later at the Pentagon. We all connected on FaceTime as much as we could to see and talk with one another from afar.

Jimmy's situation was a little more flexible. He had left the Marines and returned to school, and now he took a semester off from college so he and his lovely wife, Holly, could stay with us full-time. Having them close was a bright spot in every day. John's favorite part of our property in northern Arizona was Oak Creek, the stream that ran 365 days a year—a rarity in the dry deserts of the state. John loved Oak Creek and considered it his personal river. He had planted trees on the far side and always liked to check out what was growing and sprouting and changing.

By Christmastime, John was too weak to walk there himself, but he kept mentioning the outing he wanted to take. "I really want to go across the creek," he said.

It wouldn't be easy. At the spot where we usually crossed, the creek was about one hundred feet wide. There was no way John could walk across, and the vehicles we had weren't solid enough to carry him safely through the woods.

"Your dad was talking about the creek again," I told Jimmy one morning. We were having breakfast together in our kitchen, and Jimmy just nodded.

"I'm going to take care of this," he said.

Without any further discussion, he went into town and bought a Polaris ATV, a heavy four-wheel vehicle that can go over any kind of ground. He got mesh doors put on it so John couldn't slip out, and it had seatbelts and a roll bar, so we were good. I was so grateful that Jimmy had gotten a leave from his military duties to stay with us at the cabin. Having his support and initiative around us meant the world—and the ATV he bought was pretty great, too.

As Christmas got closer, we made plans to have a barbecue on the creek. We gathered up gear, and on a cold day, we bundled John into the new ATV and drove across the creek. We got a huge fire going and set up a bar. Everyone had cocktails and told stories and laughed. John wasn't supposed to drink, but really, what were we worried about at this point? He sipped from his drink while looking around at his favorite place, and the contentment in his eyes made all the effort worthwhile. John loved to barbecue at the creek, and even though he couldn't do it himself anymore, we set up a rotisserie and barbecued a pig.

"I know you like to be in charge, so thanks for letting me take over," Jimmy said to John.

"Well, I can still tell you everything you're doing wrong," John said with a laugh.

The pleasure of that day convinced us to keep devising ways to enjoy whatever time we could. I got John a four-wheel-drive wheelchair—sort of a beach chair with giant wheels—so he could go outside and move through the grass in the yard. As the weather got warm again, we put a little umbrella on it so he wouldn't get sunburned. He loved being out, and a couple of times, we rolled him down to the creek and invited neighbors to join us for cocktails.

Over the next months, though, John continued getting weaker. He was alert and determined, but his body failed him. One day when we were in the house, he became catastrophically ill, and we flew him by helicopter to the hospital. The doctor who met us was a lovely human being, and he explained that John's intestines had ruptured. It was another side effect of the steroid, and emergency surgery was needed that would result in a bag for his intestines.

"He may not survive it," the doctor said gently. He gave me the option of whether or not to go ahead.

John wasn't conscious enough for me to ask what he wanted to do. I knew he didn't want any excessive procedures taken—or, as he put it, "any crazy stuff done." I had promised him, too, that I wouldn't allow resuscitation. But did the current surgery fall into that category? The doctor explained that the rupture had been caused by the drugs, not by the brain tumor.

"He *could* survive it, correct?" I asked.

"He certainly could," the doctor said.

"And this isn't from the brain tumor progressing, it was caused by the drugs?"

"Correct."

I made a decision to go ahead. He would have the surgery. When he came out of it, John understood what I had done and he said he agreed. He spent quite a while in the hospital, and the event was never reported. I am grateful to the sheriff of Yavapai County and all the people of the Verde Valley for how they protected our privacy. Getting John to the hospital involved blocking a road so the helicopter could get down, calling an ambulance to bring John from our home, another roadblock, and a helicopter taking off. Nobody ever leaked a word of it. I can't thank them enough. After that surgery, we came straight back to our cabin, and we never left again.

In those final months, the press tried one trick after another to get a photo of John. Our neighbors on the hill above were offered a huge payoff to let reporters camp out on their property. They said no, slamming the door on that possibility. Still, we saw drones buzzing overhead and people standing on the ridge with telephoto lenses. I thought about how sad this game was. Why would anyone take pleasure in seeing a brave human being in decline? I finally put guards at the entrance to the property to stop the cars that tried to zoom down our dirt road and the people who showed up saying they had urgent messages, hoping to get a glimpse of John. The twenty-four-hour security helped. When I learned that helicopter companies had put our house on their tours, I just shook my head. I needed some help controlling the situation.

From the moment of John's diagnosis, I had dropped everything else in my life to be with him in the places he loved, playing nurse, doctor, pastor, loving partner, and scheduler. Now I added the role of enforcer. John wanted to keep his condition private, and I knew I could be a viper when necessary. It was necessary now. Only his closest friends and people we trusted would be allowed to come by. John wanted to collect everyone's cellphones at the door, but that seemed excessively dramatic, so I just told people to put their phones away. Visits of any sort would leave John worn out, but he still loved having people around him and engaging in conversation.

Mitt Romney came more than once. He wasn't there to talk politics, but John couldn't resist. "We need your voice in the Senate," he told Romney. "The country needs people with values again."

Mitt thanked John and said he was humbled by his confidence.

"You know me—I'm always direct," John said. They both laughed at the understatement. Later, when Mitt announced his run, I thought back to that visit and couldn't help thinking John had talked him into it.

Lindsey Graham visited a few times, as did Joe Biden and many others. I was touched by their respect for him. Afterward, they would tell the press that they had seen John McCain and offer only words of admiration.

To keep John as mobile as possible, I got him a special high-tech hospital bed. Instead of pushing, I could toggle a switch to make it go forward or backward. We joked that it could probably spin around in circles, too. Our master bedroom opens onto a patio, and I liked to steer the bed outside and sit with John, enjoying the peaceful vistas and the calming sounds of the woods. When our tranquility was broken by the blast of a helicopter or a drone overhead, I would push the button to roll him back inside, then drop the screen on the doorway so he remained out of view.

John had taught me a lot about how to live over the years. Now, in these months, he was showing all of us how to die. He knew what the outcome was going to be, and he was superhuman in some ways in facing the end with strength and resolve. John wrote his final book during this time, working with his longtime collaborator Mark Salter, and he also planned his own funeral. He discussed the details when his staff came over, and sometimes it was so painful for me that I had to leave the room. Being buried at the Naval Academy next to his old friend Chuck Larson meant the world to John, and he thought through the details of the services to be held in Phoenix, Washington, and Annapolis. He chose the people he wanted to be pallbearers and speakers, and he called many of them personally. Not surprisingly, people were often overcome with emotion at his request—and John ended up being the one offering them consolation.

Whether as a POW or a prisoner of cancer, John refused to let outside circumstances determine his responses. Over the years, he had told stories of the code he and his fellow POWs in Hanoi worked out so they could tap on the walls separating them and share news and hope. I always admired those stories. No matter how unthinkable the situation, you can maintain some control. In his final months, John wanted to celebrate a happy life well lived, rather than mourn its ending. He wouldn't be gloomy now, and he didn't want us to be, either.

Despite my own overwhelming sadness, I reminded myself that John had always been filled with exuberance—and he deserved to feel that way in his final months, too. My being gloomy wouldn't help anybody. I thought back to Meghan's wedding, a few months earlier, and the joy it had created. Throwing a wild, happy party in the midst of illness and impending death may not be a standard approach, but all of us who loved John were suffering, and we needed to feel happy for a few hours. Despite the metaphor, there is a limit to how much you can "fight" cancer. Sometimes all you can do is resolve to be cheerful and strong rather than miserable and scared.

Inspired by John's positive approach to life and death, I decided to throw a Great Gatsby party. Mostly, I wanted John to feel normal for a little bit and to remember what it was like to be the old John McCain, having fun and being at the center of a good time. I invited our closest friends from around the country and asked them to come in costume that fit the theme. They arrived to find a glamorously decorated tent with a dance floor, and after a fully served meal, the mood turned festive, with everyone dancing and swinging to the twenties-style band.

Sitting in a wheelchair, John was grateful to see everyone and the party swirling around him. Many of the guests probably sensed that this would be the last time they could talk to John, give him a hug, and tell him how important he had been to them. John delighted in the party, and he went to bed happy that night. He turned in a little earlier than the rest of us, who danced and partied on. When I got back to our room, John was sleeping, and I sat looking at him for a long time. Despite everything, he was still the man I had fallen in love with that night in Hawaii almost forty years earlier—caring, honest, and resolved. Though the twinkle in his eye had started to fade, I could still feel the energy and fire that had animated his life. I didn't want to lose him yet, but his spirit and his love would be lodged in my heart forever.

I stayed at John's side as much as I could after that. We had conversations about the future and staying strong. We talked a lot about the children and what would be best for them, and with his usual generous spirit, John was more worried about me than himself.

"There are going to be hard times and a lot of pitfalls," he said.

"You've taught me to handle anything," I reminded him.

We had been married so long that we knew each other's faults. We talked about the mistakes each of us had made and the good times we'd shared. At one point, John reached over and took my hand.

"All that really matters is how much I've loved you," he said.

"You have to know how much I've loved you, too," I said.

We didn't need to say more. We just sat in the dwindling light, our hands clasped, holding on to the love we had shared for so long and understanding that it would never end.

Three days before John died, he lapsed into a coma. I kept talking to him and bringing him outside and making sure he could be surrounded by the birds and sounds he loved—until my neighbor who is a doctor pointed out that the end was near. I suppose I knew, but when the time arrives, it is still a shock. I will never forget those last moments of John's life when we were on the deck of our house, with

Frank Sinatra's "My Way" playing in the background, and a hawk flew by as my husband drew his final breath. You are never ready for the person you love to be gone. For me, it was like going into a foggy tunnel. Once inside, it was disorienting and unfamiliar, a place I didn't want to be.

The moment on the deck had a mystical feel to me—but then the reality of John's death hit hard. I stumbled inside and found the clothes I had put aside to take with me for the funeral. Fortunately, John's closest staff had prepared everything else. They had SUVs and a hearse staged in Sedona, waiting for the call that the time had come. Within an hour, they were pulling up to our cabin. Our closest friends and family were with us, except for Jack, who was still deployed in Afghanistan. We had been trying to get him home, but it was difficult. Everyone agreed that he needed to be out of Afghanistan before the press knew about John's death and tried to find him, but Jack didn't want any special treatment. A commanding officer finally informed him that he needed to get to the airport where an airplane was waiting.

Just before Jack got on the plane, I reached him by phone and had to break the news to him that his father had died. Jack had said his goodbyes in person the last time he was home, but I could hear the shock in his voice at the finality of the news. Picturing him alone and far away, with a long trip ahead accompanied only by sadness, I desperately wanted to be able to hug him. But on this day, nothing was the way I would have chosen.

As we prepared to leave the cabin, I went into autopilot, trying to appear strong and in control, even though I wasn't feeling it at all. I knew I had to hold myself together for the good of our family. It would have done nobody any good to see me coming apart. Meghan had collapsed in sobs, and I tried to help her. Everybody handles grief in their own way. A few days earlier, she had seemed almost angry that I was trying so hard to be stoic and contained.

"Mommy, you're not showing any emotion. You don't even cry," she had said.

"I do cry, and sometimes I cry more than I want to," I said. "It's just not when you can see it."

She would bring up the subject again after one of the funeral services, but with more admiration this time. "I don't know how you're doing this, Mom," she said. "I can't keep the control that you do."

"I want to be strong for everyone in the nation and the world who is mourning your father," I said. "I have to do that whether I want to or not. This funeral is more than me and you and our family."

Meghan's suffering was on the surface. Later that week, the whole world saw her grief-stricken face as John's casket was taken into the U.S. Capitol, and they noted her fiery strength as she gave a powerful eulogy at the National Cathedral. I steeled myself enough to keep my anguish and pain private.

After the funeral, I had many people say to me, "You were so strong. How did you do it?" Well, you just do it. John was a staunch and determined person, and he wouldn't have wanted me to be a mess. I had spent many decades regarding the strong McCain women as my role models. Now I was one of them.

But as we all left the cabin together in those first hours after John's death, I wasn't sure how long my resolve would hold. The first ride was more emotional than I could have imagined. As we reached the top of our long driveway, a crowd had already gathered to say goodbye, and as we traveled toward Phoenix, the crowds kept growing. How had they all heard the news so quickly and figured out where we would be? I still don't know the answers, but at each step in the next few days, my wonderment grew with the size of each new gathering. I was overwhelmed by the outpouring of admiration and respect and love from around the world.

The next day, John lay in state at the Arizona State Capitol, which remained open into the night as throngs of people filed through to pay their respects. "Only John McCain could rig a birthday celebration for himself like this," said our longtime friend Rick Davis with a smile. The day would have been John's eighty-second birthday. Rick's making a joke as John would have done was yet another way of handling grief.

At the service the next day at North Phoenix Baptist Church, John's dear friend Joe Biden was among those who spoke. "My name is Joe Biden," he began, looking down at his notes on the lectern and trying to stay composed. When a murmur of laughter passed through the church at his humble introduction, he looked up with a smile. "I'm a Democrat. And I loved John McCain."

John and Joe did love each other, and they had gotten to say so while John could still hear the words himself. As a culmination of their many years working with (and against) each other in the Senate, Biden had presented an award to John at the National Constitution Center in Philadelphia back in October. He'd praised John's strength and their long and devoted friendship, and I thought it was a great gift that so many people could share their admiration and love for John that night. In return, John gave what would turn out to be his final speech, a poetic ode to the ideals of America and the power of trying to create a future that is better than the past. He described as unpatriotic those who refuse the obligations of international leadership "for the sake of some half-baked, spurious nationalism cooked up by people who would rather find scapegoats than solve problems." He called himself the luckiest guy on earth to have served America's cause of freedom and equal justice.

Now Joe gave an emotional and passionate eulogy for his friend and colleague, dabbing at his eyes with his handkerchief more than once. He told moving stories about growing up in the Senate with John. "Character is destiny," he said. "John had character." He promised our family that instead of the stabbing pain and hollowness we were feeling now, we would eventually be filled only with the happy images of John's life. Joe knew, of course—his son Beau had died of the same terrible disease.

Thousands of people packed the church for the funeral, and then we flew to Washington, D.C., where hundreds of military personnel, including the secretary of defense, were waiting for us at the airport, standing in the heat and saluting, along with members of Congress. I tried to acknowledge them, but I could hardly speak. Over to one side, I noticed John's staff, standing patiently and quietly to pay their respects. I veered from our path and walked the three hundred feet over to see them and grasp their hands. Their kindness was a great comfort to me amidst the emotion of John leaving his beloved Arizona for the last time.

In Washington that night, I girded myself for what was ahead. In the morning, we left with a motorcade to take John to lie in state in the Rotunda of the U.S. Capitol. The privilege of lying in state has been awarded to just a dozen presidents, including Abraham Lincoln and Ronald Reagan, and a few statesmen and military leaders, and it is one of the deepest honors that the United States can give someone.

As we got out of the car at the Capitol, the weather felt steamy, like it was about to rain. We were ushered in through a side door, took an elevator up, and were led outside to stand at the top of the long staircase. As we waited under the portico by the huge pillars of the Capitol, the rain did start to fall. My children and I watched as a military honor guard took the flag-draped casket from the hearse and smoothly carried it toward the staircase—and then they ascended, one step at a time, with diligence, determination, and precision. Such strong men. John had once been just like them. I covered my heart with my hand as the casket stopped next to me. Then, we followed the casket into the Capitol.

Inside, senators and representatives from both parties awaited our arrival. The packed crowd also included cabinet members, Supreme Court justices, and the vice president. I had attended many services and ceremonies, but this was more stately and overwhelming than anything I could imagine. John had never been president, but he was being treated and honored as if he were a head of state. Later, I discovered that the major networks covered the farewell to John as a breaking news event, with extensive coverage and commentary. Even outlets that had challenged John's positions during his lifetime understood that his patriotism, honor, and dedication to country set him apart.

"You could never doubt that this man was a patriot," said one of the network reporters who covered the ceremony live for ABC.

John's mother, Roberta, age 106, sat next to Meghan during the speeches that followed, reaching out to hold her hand and offer comfort. After the public comments, everyone in the room had a chance to walk by the casket and say goodbye to John. I was led forward to start the procession. I clasped my hands on top of the casket and dropped my head for a moment, saying the goodbye that was in my heart. Then I whispered, "I love you." There was nothing more to say.

Each of the children came up for their turn. Then, slowly, all the dignitaries in the room followed. Once they had said their goodbyes, the room opened up to the general public. I stayed nearby for a long time. I think John would have been happiest to know how many people from around the country, of all political positions, in all walks of life, cared enough to make the trip to say goodbye. The Rotunda seemed so vast and formal, and when night came, I didn't want to leave him there alone. Then I thought, *There are so many people here. Navy officers are standing guard. John would be happy.*

On Saturday, we walked in a processional to the Vietnam Veterans Memorial, where I lay a wreath in John's memory. As happened over and over through the funeral events, I walked holding Jimmy's arm on one side of me and Jack's on the other. My handsome, brave sons were the rocks I needed, Jack standing tall in his Navy dress whites and Jimmy in his Army dress blues. From there, another honor guard carried John's casket into the Washington National Cathedral for the powerful and extraordinary memorial. I knew who would be there, but I was still moved to see leaders from around the world who had come to say goodbye. The row of former presidents and vice presidents of the United States seemed to stretch on and on. The honorary pallbearers John had chosen included members of both parties, business executives including Michael Bloomberg, a Russian named Vladimir Kara-Murza who had stood up against Putin, and our longtime friend Warren Beatty. It was John's final statement of bipartisanship.

"We have always had so much more in common with each other than disagreement," John had written in a final letter to them.

In the ceremony details, the descriptions of each of the pallbearers began with the simple word "Friend." The same was true for the speakers, including Presidents George W. Bush and Barack Obama. For John, friendship came first, and political ideology could be challenged and discussed. Some commentators would later suggest that given the administration that had taken over, John's funeral was a farewell of sorts to the less-divisive America that he believed in and fought for his entire career, the one that was strong and admired across the globe. We all hoped John's America would emerge again.

In his eulogy, President Bush said that, above all, "John detested the abuse of power. He could not abide bigots and swaggering despots. There was something deep inside him that made him stand up for the little guy—to speak for forgotten people in forgotten places." President Obama said that when he and John met often in the White House to talk about politics and policy, neither of them ever doubted that they were on the same team. He went on to say that he "never saw John treat anyone differently because of their race, religion, or gender." Those words in particular penetrated my fog of grief, and I thought, *How true.*

I managed to stay composed through the accolades, the memories, and the beautiful, soaring words of the people John had chosen to speak. But at the end of the service, as opera singer Renée Fleming offered an exquisite rendition of "Danny Boy," I couldn't hold back tears any longer. I leaned against Jack, who put a comforting arm around me. John often sat on the porch of our cabin and listened to "Danny Boy," the music drifting over Oak Creek. It seemed so unfair that the music was now drifting over his flag-draped coffin. John would have liked to hear Renée singing to him. He would have liked it a lot.

In the midst of the grief, the memorials, the services, and the effort to stay strong, I didn't think much about eating or drinking. After the National Cathedral, several friends accompanied me back to my apartment in downtown Washington. I was shaken and probably hungry and someone suggested we go over to Oyamel, a restaurant right on our block. The owner José Andrés is a great friend of mine. I admire not only his terrific food but his work to bring healthy food to people in crisis.

Soon we had fifty or so people, including some who had been at the funeral and many McCainiacs who had worked on John's campaigns over the years. Their vivaciousness and love of John was enough to lift my spirits for a little while. The younger ones lifted some liquid spirits, too—with all kinds of tequilas flowing through the night. I didn't join them for that, but I appreciated the cocoon of comfort and energy that surrounded me in the restaurant. I managed to eat a little bit, too.

I woke up the next morning and tried to prepare myself for the final goodbye. On our drive to the Naval Academy, I looked out at the streets of Annapolis. Once again, people had lined up along the route—waving flags, saluting, and holding children in their arms to share the moment. Inside the Naval Academy chapel, I listened to the final eulogies. Jack, with his own young son watching, spoke movingly of his dad's example, saying John wanted his children to find their own path and live adventurously and bravely in service to something greater than themselves. It occurred to me that the huge outpouring of the previous few days was proof of the power of that vision. It's easy to get caught up in our own needs and desires and personal experiences, but we all understand somewhere in our hearts the value of seeing beyond ourselves. In paying homage to John, we were honoring a man who had been able to live with a bigger view and a greater purpose.

The Naval Academy chapel was packed with midshipmen in their dress whites, and however sad the moment, it felt right. John was coming home to the people and place he loved. A horse-drawn caisson carried his casket to the Naval Academy Cemetery as the midshipmen lined the route, saluting. Fighter planes in a missing-man formation flew overhead. We buried John next to a longtime friend and classmate, Admiral Chuck Larson. Through my tears at the grave site, I thought of the poem Jimmy had read the day before at the National Cathedral. It was the same verse by Robert Louis Stevenson that John had read at his own father's ceremony:

Glad did I live and gladly die. . . .
Here he lies where he longed to be;
Home is the sailor, home from the sea.

The next day, we were due to leave. I left our apartment in the morning, and as I stepped into the hot, sticky Washington air, I thought to myself, *How am I getting home?* Everything for the funeral had been so carefully orchestrated, and now what? I vaguely remembered that when General Mattis had handed me the American flag at the cemetery, he mentioned that there would be an airplane at my disposal. Now someone got me into a car, and when we drove to an airport, I was overwhelmed to see Air Force Two waiting. A group of naval officers in their dress whites were gathered outside the plane before I boarded. Their grace and respect brought me to tears once more, but this time, I was also able to smile. Many of these officers had served with John or guided him on trips around the world. They were all there to say goodbye one more time.

After thanking the officers, I stepped onto the plane with some friends and family. I was going home—but home would forever be a different place.

CHAPTER 14

Moving Forward

In the first weeks after the funeral, a group of Jimmy's friends in Phoenix checked up on me on a regular basis. I had known most of them since they were kids, and now these young adults had decided that I shouldn't be left alone. I suspect Jimmy organized a schedule, but he never admitted it. Most days, someone would stop by to have coffee or bring lunch. Then, later, another friend would take me to Jimmy's house or organize a dinner out. Their attentiveness and caring meant a lot.

But the bottom line is, at night, the door closes and you're alone. Some evenings I would think I heard John in the house, and the dog would start barking as if she heard him, too. It was hard to process. For thirty-eight years, we had spent plenty of time apart, but I never felt lonely because I knew the person I loved would return. John could be traveling in Vietnam or I might be in the Congo, but there remained an invisible string between us that I could tug anytime. He was just a phone call or a plane ride away. Now when I tugged that string, I could still feel his presence, but I had the shock of knowing that he would never again walk in through the door.

Our cabin up north had always been a place to escape to and find comfort, but now I couldn't imagine going there. Every spot was filled with memories of John's last year. I needed the painful images of illness and death to fade. Too much of the final months had been about watching John decline.

People often tell you that in the first year after a spouse dies, you shouldn't make any big changes in your life. I can see the reason for that advice. You're shaken, you're not thinking straight, you can't really envision the future. I understood all that. But two months after John died, I decided to leave the apartment where we had been living for the previous ten years and buy a house in our old neighborhood in Phoenix. The wide tree-lined street where I had lived for much of my life always felt like home to me, no matter where else I lived or traveled. It was a big change and a big move, and it was exactly the right thing to do. I guess you have to know yourself and not always follow the rules. I knew that I needed a home of my own that would give me comfort.

The sprawling ranch-style house had adobe and teal adornments and a tile roof, and the huge grounds included a swimming pool and a guesthouse. I loved everything about the whole setting. I moved in, and in short order, the house looked like I had been there forever. I hung family pictures on the walls and tossed blankets with the Navy insignia on couches. Mementos from John's campaigns and travels dotted the bookshelves, and a guest bedroom displayed Navy uniforms and honors from four generations of the McCain family. The ceremonial swords from John's grandfather and Jack were enclosed in a glass box and hung on the wall. We've never been able to find John's sword. The big kitchen opened to a large family room where my friends and family could casually flop down in front of a big-screen TV—or turn around and watch me doing the one thing I like to do in the kitchen, baking bread.

I had discussed my idea of moving with John toward the end of his life, and he was all for it. We had bought the condo to make security easier when we were in town, but John knew how much our old neighborhood meant to me. Other people, though, seemed appalled that I would even think about moving so quickly. After a death, everybody has an opinion about what you should be doing. Most of it is well-meaning, but I don't think there are any prescriptions for getting over grief and loss. If you are the one grieving, the only advice is to follow your heart. For everyone else, be supportive and don't make judgments. The move that seemed like a mistake to others turned out to be absolutely the right thing for me.

After the funeral, I had assumed I would go back to being a private citizen who the press didn't pay much attention to. But one day shortly after I moved in, a friend called and told me about a story in that day's *Arizona Republic* that gave my new home address.

"You're kidding," I said.

"I wish I were."

I found the article and was about to call the editor, but I checked in first with one of my longtime staff members who said that she would make the call for me. "You're going to be too angry," she said. "Let me do it."

"Please tell them that I understand and believe in freedom of the press, but putting the address of my new house in the newspaper was simply wrong," I said, trying to keep my voice calm.

"He'll say it's public record," she pointed out.

"That's different than publishing it so anyone can find me. I'm newly widowed and living alone. My husband was a very famous man. They have endangered my safety and put me at risk."

"Okay, you're right. What if he asks what you'd like them to do?"

"Tell them that they could stay out of my life going forward," I said. "How about that?"

John and I had had our differences with the newspaper in the past, but printing my new address—on the front page, no less—couldn't be considered politics or public interest. The house was on a wide main street, so I called a contractor to put up a gate at the driveway. Unfortunately, in the weeks to come, I found that I couldn't wall myself off from some of the other intrusions on our family. Trump became oddly obsessed with attacking my husband. Our family wanted to grieve privately, but Trump seemed determined to keep John alive—as his personal villain. In tweets and speeches he attacked John with innuendo and outright lies. When it reached a crescendo at a rally in Ohio in March 2019, seven months after John died, senators from both parties finally spoke out. Republican senator Johnny Isakson from Georgia called the president's comments about John "deplorable." But the president didn't stop.

"Trump is the ultimate weakling to attack someone seven months after he's passed away," one of my friends said. "He's the definition of a coward."

I fully agreed with her sentiment, and I think most people did, too. When you use a pathetic deferment for "bone spurs" to avoid serving your country, you give up the right to question anyone's heroism. But however baseless, cowardly, and misguided a president's comments may be, they have an effect. Nasty comments proliferated on Twitter as some of his followers echoed the president and tried to undermine John's name. I wondered how many of the attackers had ever served in the military or taken any personal risks for their country. It was a lot easier to go on social media and speak rudely about John, one of the most patriotic and honorable men of his generation, than to actually put on a uniform to support the greater ideals of America.

Meghan was the one person in our family who spoke out. During the fracas in March, she pointed out that the president "spends his weekend obsessing over great men because he knows it and I know it and all of you know it—he will never be a great man." I tried to stay above the fray, but when I got a profane and hate-filled message on Facebook one day from a woman I didn't know, I suddenly exploded. The coarse cruelty of her saying she was glad my husband was dead and obscenely suggesting how my daughter should die stunned me.

I went on Twitter and posted a screenshot that showed her message. I explained why I was making it public: "I want to make sure all of you could see how kind and loving a stranger can be. I'm posting her note for her family and friends [to] see." The moment I posted it, I thought, *I'm sorry if you disagree, John. But I had to draw the line.*

I didn't expect my post to make news, but it got worldwide attention. The hugely positive response to what I'd done made me feel vindicated. Nasty voices were hard to ignore, but maybe they were ultimately outnumbered by people who still believed in civility. I didn't get in the dirt with the woman who posted the nastiness or call her names. I just let her speak for herself. I wanted people to see that words have consequences. There should be a simple rule for social media—or, in fact, any kind of communication. If you would be ashamed for the world to know what you said, don't say it.

Jack and Jimmy didn't talk to me much about their reaction to the president's attacks on their dad. They were both in the military, and I know how hard it was for them to try to square the commander in chief's regular scorn for the military with their deep belief in service and honor. One event seemed almost surreal. In May 2019, the White House insisted that the name of the warship USS *John S. McCain* be covered when the president made a brief visit to a naval base in Japan. The great ship had been named for John's father and grandfather, both important Navy admirals, and it was rededicated with John added as a namesake shortly before his death. Three generations of brave naval McCains. Our son Jack makes it four. The president didn't want to face their memory or their name.

When the news broke, Meghan texted me. *Please tell me this story isn't true.*

I'll try to find out, I promised.

My friends in Washington made some inquiries, and I had to report back that it was indeed true. The ship was out of service and couldn't be moved, so the Navy draped a tarp to keep Trump from having to see the name. Then it got even worse. We learned that the sailors aboard the USS *John S. McCain* hadn't been invited to hear the president speak because he might get upset seeing the McCain name embroidered on their caps. Some who did show up were turned away. I couldn't believe it. John had stared down bullets and torture, and now we had a president who was afraid of embroidery? Showing such disrespect for those who boldly and bravely serve our country would be unacceptable in any circumstances. Doing it on behalf of the commander in chief makes it fully unfathomable.

The controversy swirled for days. The Navy denied that it had covered the ship, then they admitted it and apologized. The White House said it had never ordered the Navy to hide the ship—until *The Wall Street Journal* uncovered an email from the administration directing that the USS *John S. McCain* be out of sight during the president's visit. Apparently the president's sycophants had given the order, after all. People not associated with the military might have found it just one more presidential outrage, but it struck deep at the heart of our family.

I texted back and forth with my children about how we should respond. Ultimately, we decided to say nothing. The complete dishonor of the act was obvious to most Americans. My phone lit up with texts from friends in and out of government wanting to make sure that I was okay. Yes, I could cope. To me, the bigger question was whether our country could survive the constant undermining of the heroes it most needs.

As the presidential pettifoggery unfolded, I kept thinking about another far more significant incident with the USS *John S. McCain*. In August 2017, the ship collided with a civilian tanker near

Singapore, and there were many casualties. John had just gotten his terminal cancer diagnosis, and he and I were both overwhelmed trying to understand what was ahead. It was hard to think or talk about anything else. But the night of the collision, John put aside his personal sorrows to focus on giving comfort and condolences to others. He sat at our kitchen table and called the families of the ten sailors who lost their lives on the ship. I stayed with him at the table, listening in awe. It remains one of my most poignant memories. The families were surprised to hear from John, and most expressed gratitude for his call. The conversations couldn't have been easy, but in offering strength to others, John seemed to gain more for himself. Perhaps giving kindness and empathy to others is the best way to help yourself, too.

John couldn't have imagined the extent of the political morass after his death. But in the year that he was ill, he tried to prepare me on a personal level for life after he was gone. He urged me to stay strong, keep our family together, and use my voice for good. "People will try to take advantage of your name and use you," he said, "but you'll be wise to them. You're too strong to let that happen."

I'd faced a similar situation after my dad died in 2000. He was a wonderful man and skilled at building his business. By the time he died, the company he founded was one of the largest Anheuser-Busch beer distributorships in the country. John's memorial services had been stately and magnificent, but my dad is the only person I know who had a Clydesdale at his funeral. It was one of the things he wanted, and the church was kind enough to allow the horse to stand proudly on the lawn outside.

Not long after my dad's death, the brewery made a move on me. I had taken over as chairman of Hensley & Co., and I got a call that some top executives at Anheuser-Busch would like to meet with me at their headquarters in Saint Louis. When I arrived, I was met by August Busch III, the chairman of the board and great-grandson of the company's founder. I had known him for much of my life, and we sat down in a big boardroom. It quickly became clear that he wanted to buy the company from under me. We had a franchise, and while the brewery does have the right to remove it if the owner is misman-aging the company or doing something illegal, none of that was the case for us. Rather, we had a very profitable distributorship, and they wanted it.

Throughout the meeting, August and the other executives were polite. They suggested that running a beverage company probably wasn't a job that a woman like me would want to do. Surely I would want to sell the company, and if I did, they would be first in line to buy it. They were prepared to make an offer.

"I have no intention of selling," I told them. "I also don't appreciate your assumption that because I'm a woman, I would accept your offer."

"Oh, we just know how busy you are with your husband and your life as a political spouse," one of them said.

I wasn't buying their explanation—or selling the company—but it was all a little unnerving to me. Apparently, there had been other cases around the country where the widow or heirs did sell to get some money and avoid future headaches, but my dad had always made sure that I felt like an integral part of the company, and I wasn't giving it up. Not only was Hensley & Co. very profitable, it had kept my dad involved in the community and part of the fiber of Phoenix, Arizona. My plan was to keep it in the family.

"You understand about legacy," I said to August Busch. "I'd like my children to have the same option to join the company as you did—and as your children will."

Since one of his four children was at the meeting, August simply nodded. I'd spoken a little more harshly than I had intended, but I wanted to make my position crystal clear. They were way off base in thinking that a woman wouldn't want to take over the enterprise. I got an attorney involved, and they eventually backed down. I think they knew they had met their match in me.

I didn't have any issues like that after John's death, but I felt a huge drive to work as hard as I could to make the McCain Institute a world leader in the areas John cared about: national security, rule of law, and next-generation leaders. During the first years of the institute, John had been gracious enough to make half of its mission focus on humanitarian issues, the concerns that most drove me.

After the 2008 election, I had learned the value of jumping back into bigger causes to put your own losses in perspective. Now with this greatest personal loss of all, I knew I had to get right back to work—if only because John insisted that I pick up again as quickly as I could. "Don't you sit around and be sad," he said more than once in those final months. "You get back to work, right back at it."

Hearing his voice in my head, I revved up again as quickly as I could. John was right: Nothing good comes from sitting around and thinking too much. You need to move forward, and having the structure of the McCain Institute for support made it easier. I needed to get back and I wanted to get back to work. I had become known over the years for my focus on human trafficking, and that was where I turned my attention. It's not the easiest topic to discuss. There is a certain "ick" factor when you bring it up. People don't want to think about what's happening around the world and in their own towns to those they may even see or know. After drug trafficking, sex and labor trafficking is the world's largest criminal industry, but even now, the problem is more often hidden than discussed.

I got my first hint of the problem a couple of years after bringing Bridget home, when I had a chance to visit Calcutta and meet with Mother Teresa. I wanted to show her Bridget's picture and thank her for all the good she had done. After meeting her and visiting another orphanage, I was on my way to the airport when I stopped to buy some sari material for Bridget. As I went to pay, I heard some rumbling under the floorboards.

"What's going on?" I asked the owner.

"It's just my family," he said. "They live below."

It seemed plausible, and I proceeded to pay for the cloth. The noise continued, and noticing gaps between the floorboards, I took a quick peek down and saw rows of little eyes peering back at me. My heart jumped. There were far too many little faces for the children to be from one family. Something was clearly wrong. I didn't have a name for it, though, and there was nothing I could do at that moment.

I got in the airplane and returned home to my nice house and lovely family—but I couldn't forget those eyes. Heaven knew how many other children were suffering in similar conditions. It was hard to find anyone who would talk to me about it or discuss what we might do. So I read a whole lot and started trying to figure out the problem. I came to understand that unscrupulous people around the world took children from their homes for slave labor and for sex. The children were often moved from one location to another and tossed away when they were no longer needed. I thought it happened only in places like Bangladesh or Calcutta—but I soon discovered that it was a problem close to home.

Labor trafficking isn't just about the immigrant worker in the field—it's the maid who works too long and the food service worker stuck in the back of the truck and the quiet manicurist at the nail salon. Many people you rely on every day are trapped in situations not of their choosing. We need to find a way to treat people better and more fairly, and find a sane way to make sure they are cared for and not exploited. With sex trafficking, the issue is even more discomforting. I've heard the girls referred to as prostitutes, but how could that possibly be the right term for a twelve-year-old girl held against her will and forced to have sex? The problem of luring in vulnerable young girls and moving them around for sex and money is happening in this country, right now, under all of our noses.

The Defense Advanced Research Projects Agency, a unit of the U.S. Department of Defense, can track the routes where sex trafficking occurs. It often flourishes around some of the biggest and seemingly most wholesome events in the country. I confronted the National Football League in 2015 when the Super Bowl came to Phoenix, explaining that the game has become one of the biggest venues for human trafficking on the planet. The state hotel and tourism agencies agreed to take part in an awareness campaign, and I asked the NFL to get involved with anti-trafficking ads that could be shown on television during games. The NFL execs, famous for denying the concussions their own players suffer, wanted no part of it.

"Could we join together for a press conference to at least acknowledge the issue?" I asked.

"Our players are not involved in this problem at all," they said.

"Fine, but your players are influential and could make a difference in raising awareness," I explained.

"We're not going to do it," they said.

The day after the Super Bowl, a former player who had been in Phoenix to cover the game for the NFL Network was arrested for soliciting two women who were quite possibly victims of trafficking, and assaulting one of them. He was in the Hall of Fame, too. I didn't show up at the NFL offices to say "I told you so"—but I sure wanted to. The next year, when the Super Bowl was held in Miami, several players participated in a thirty-second anti-trafficking-campaign video that played in airports, hotels, and even in the backseats of Uber sedans.

The NFL isn't the only target. Organized sex-trafficking rings target any sporting event that attracts big crowds, including the Final Four, the Masters, the NBA playoffs, and the opening day of baseball.

Any big gathering that involves a lot of money can become a focal point, from auto shows to professional conventions for doctors, lawyers, or insurance salesmen. I raised some political hackles when I pointed out the trafficking that takes place around the Republican National Convention. Come on, did anyone really think it was just the Democrats? Nobody is immune.

Humanitarian agencies and law enforcement have to work together to identify the problem spots and try to find a coordinated solution. We often identify the wrong person—the young woman—as the criminal. The number one person at fault is the customer. Number two is the pimp who is moving them around. The fourteen-year-old girl who is a runaway from an abusive home, or who was lured in by a pimp in a mall telling her how beautiful she was, needs to be protected by the Justice Department.

After John's death, I stepped up my efforts with the institute's backing. One of our priorities was to encourage international coordination and convince governments to take an active role in breaking up the trafficking rings. I went to Hong Kong, Jakarta, Manila, Rome, and Miami—and that was just a start. I met with victims of trafficking who had been rescued in Burma and spoke at a nursing association meeting in Singapore. My reception in Singapore was different than it had been just a couple of years earlier. On the previous trip, a former ambassador had gotten irate when I tried to bring up the issue.

"There's no need for this discussion," she said. "We have no problem with trafficking here."

"It's been documented," I told her. "May I show you the findings?"

She didn't want to hear about it, which wasn't a complete surprise. It's always easier for officials to look the other way than admit a problem. My job was simply to call attention to the issue, so I was glad to be invited to Singapore this time to let the nurses know what they should be looking for and how they could help.

As I threw myself into my travels, I worked to raise money so the institute could expand its reach on human rights and human dignity. For the first time ever, I had no particular reason to go home. Being on the road felt both right and comfortable. Leaders around the world knew and admired John, and many of them were happy to let me come and talk to them about the problems and hear my views. I'm not an elected official, so I'm careful in these meetings, but I always remind myself that this is not politics—I am speaking for the children of the world suffering from heinous exploitation. The children who every individual and government should be protecting.

Every year on my birthday, I take a trip with a group of my closest women friends. It's always fun and rollicking, but when we make the itinerary, we also include at least one stop with a humanitarian bent. Lately, these learning stops have focused on human trafficking.

The year after John died, we flew to Southeast Asia and boarded the Eastern and Oriental Express for a three-night adventure. The train goes through three countries and makes several stops, but much of the fascination comes from simply being on board. John and I had taken the kids on the same trip a number of years earlier, and he had been moved by the stop at the bridge on the river Kwai. The bridge was built by Allied prisoners during World War II and was made famous by the old movie starring Alec Guinness and William Holden. Though the movie shows the bridge being destroyed at the end, it still stands. Thousands of POWs died in the dangerous forced labor of building the bridge, and two huge cemeteries nearby bear their graves. Visiting years later with my friends, we walked through the small museum that tells the story of the bridge, and we laid a wreath at the cemetery.

We all had fun on our three-night trip—looking out the window at the fascinating scenery and indulging in the stylish onboard meals. We laughed a lot and played card games and had a girls' good time on the classic luxury train. But the laughter stopped when we got to

Bangkok and I took my friends to a small outlying village known as Little Girl Town. As the nickname suggests, it is essentially a place for sex tourism. We had dinner and then met with a local police official and asked him to allow us to walk around.

"You don't have to do that," he said. "I can answer your questions."

"Thanks, but we'd like to walk through," I said.

He hesitated and looked uncertain for a moment. He didn't want us to see what was going on, but he couldn't think of a reason to stop us. He left quickly and we got started on our walk. The tourists we saw were mostly Caucasian men from Europe and the United States who were there to make their sex purchases. Girls in their late teens were dancing in the bars, and the guys—their pimps—stood outside making deals for them. As we continued walking, music filled the street. A little farther on, we saw young girls aged twelve or thirteen, huddled together. They stood quietly and had blank, staring eyes. They had obviously been drugged and now waited to be taken away for whatever their purchasers had in mind. Shaken, we kept walking and encountered tiny girls in cute little white dresses standing on the street. The youngest was barely four years old and the oldest was probably seven. All of them were drugged into a near-stupor. As I stood there, I watched one of the girls being sold.

"How old do you want and what do you need her to do?" I heard the pimp ask.

One of my friends who was standing with me blanched. "I think I'm going to vomit," she said, covering her face with her hands.

We went around the corner to Little Boy Alley, and here we saw a similar scene, but now with little boys and teenagers. Many were sitting at tables with old white guys who had their arms around them and their hands at their pants. There was nothing sexy about the tableau—it all felt menacing and creepy. I later heard that on that particular street, boys are sold for snuff games, which means that one of the children I saw that night might have died for someone's sick fun. Their images haunt and horrify me. I don't know how anyone can turn away.

When we finished our walk, we tried to talk to the police chief about what we had seen. But we quickly realized that it wasn't news to him—he was complicit. Back at our hotel, my girlfriends and I talked long into the night about what we had seen, our anger boiling over. They were fired up and furious, and I knew that the emotions would lead to action.

"I'm going to start raising money for your cause as soon as I get home," one of my friends said, her voice brimming with passion.

"Well, that's one reason I bring you," I said wryly.

I often hear the complaint that certain politicians care about protecting children until they're born and turn their backs afterward. But seeing the injustices in the world with your own eyes changes you forever. As decent human beings, we need to take stock in our children and speak up for those who can't safeguard themselves. Every individual and country needs to step in and fight against trafficking.

For years, I felt like a Chihuahua on this issue, biting at people's ankles and trying to get attention. But now the discussions are happening all over the world, and I find it enormously encouraging. If I've had an impact on making it part of a mainstream understanding, then I can feel proud of having done my part.

CHAPTER 15

⁓∞⁓

Making a Better World

For Christmas the year John died, I invited a few people to join me at Turtle Island in Fiji. John and I had been going there since before we had children, and we even joked that Meghan had been a Turtle baby. Over the years, we continued to visit, sometimes by ourselves and often at Christmas with the children. Turtle Island became a faraway retreat that also felt like home.

Each night, we would eat together with the visitors staying in nearby villas, and the style was so easygoing that we often didn't even wear shoes. The conversations were always spirited, and the camaraderie was just the kind of thing that John reveled in. He loved getting to know exotic places, and he connected easily with the locals and natives. They in turn adored him. When the kids were little, our whole family stayed together in a villa and woke up every morning looking out at the blue lagoon.

Before going this time, I took some dirt from John's grave site at the Naval Academy and put it in a plastic bag to bring with me. Once in Fiji, I took it out to a tree that John and I had planted on the island some twenty-five years earlier. I dug a little hole and scattered the dirt so that John could forever be part of the South Pacific. People who knew John from our years on the island did a little ceremony for him, and we all said goodbye.

The group I had brought included friends as well as the stalwart caregivers who had so lovingly tended John in the last year. I don't know how I could have survived those months without them. The trip was a way to say that they had become part of our extended family.

One night around Christmas, we decided we would all dress up in traditional South Pacific garb, so we got coconut bras and grass skirts and had dinner on the beach. John would surely have loved the fun and laughter and the warm feeling of being together on the island. I hoped that in future Christmases, Turtle Island would be a place I could gather our children and grandchildren, because John's spirit would always be there.

In his months of saying goodbye and preparing me to go on without him, John asked me to do two things: Take care of his legacy and take care of our family. It is important to me to represent what John stood for, including his dedication to civility and dignity and honor. I had to stay above the fray and try to show that America could be better than the angry, divisive country its leaders were starting to encourage.

I thought often of how John and I raised our children to take responsibility for themselves and the bigger world, and I think parents can still do that. Raising children with a sense of duty and honor and values takes time and effort. When our children were growing up, John made sure that we not only had dinner together every Sunday, but also that we talked about important issues around the table. We would discuss topics from everyday life and challenge the children to decide what was the good thing to do. We tried to exhibit proper behavior, but we were also quick to admit when we made mistakes. We were only human, and that's okay. We took the children to military parades and the Army-Navy football game because it is fun showing kids that good values can have an exciting side, too. Modeling leadership and service doesn't have to be just about the military. I think schools and parents should be more direct about encouraging service of all kinds and helping children and teenagers find something that they can contribute to the greater good.

Jack and Jimmy went to an all-boys high school that had a service policy called Men for Others. It was one of the many things John and I admired about the school, but we would often hear other parents grumbling and objecting to activities that took place on a Saturday. *Wait a minute*, I thought. *Let's figure out what's important here!* It should be worth messing up your weekend schedule a little to raise children who are not just intelligent but also good human beings who care about their community.

On the first anniversary of John's death, I wrote an op-ed for *The Washington Post* urging all Americans to take a pledge of civility and commit to causes larger than themselves. I urged members of Congress to return to the position John embodied of open hearts and the possibility of compromise. I also think it is deeply important for all of us to demonstrate kindness and decency in the places where we have influence. You can start within your own home and expand outward— perhaps make friends with a neighbor you disagree with or try to understand people you have never met whose positions are different from yours. For America to be the country it always could be, we need more compassion, we need more empathy, and we need less bullying.

John insisted that we have a party on the first anniversary of his death, with the music from his favorite playlist filling the air and the company of people who had worked and campaigned for him throughout his life. We always joked that we held Hotel California parties—because with the McCainiacs, once you checked in, you never checked out. I got through the anniversary and John's birthday with the warmth and support of our close friends, and I helped raise a flag in the state capital in John's honor. With a year gone by, the heaviest grief had started to subside, though I still found myself in tears at private, unexpected moments. John had occupied such a huge space in my life that I would never stop missing him. All I could do was learn to live with the heartbreak of loss and take comfort that as I suffered through fewer impossibly bad days, I could make the rest of the time richer and more meaningful.

A few weeks earlier, I had gone to Japan with Jimmy and Jack and Jack's wife, Renee, to celebrate the twenty-fifth anniversary of the commissioning of the USS *John S. McCain*. After all the nonsense surrounding the ship in the previous weeks, it was going back to sea after being in dry dock for repairs. This was the first time I had been aboard since John was added as a namesake. The ship's commander, Micah Murphy, unveiled an exquisite portrait of John as a young man that would hang on the ship. It had been painted by John's chief of staff, Truman Anderson. The commander gave me a plaque to memorialize the commissioning. The ceremony moved me to tears.

Our trip to the USS *John S. McCain* had been planned for a while, and that it came so soon after controversy was just a coincidence. Micah had been a legislative fellow of John's, so I already knew him to be a consummate naval officer. He never said a word about the problem or disclosed anything he had learned, and I felt it inappropriate to ask.

Walking around the ship, I felt so happy to be there and see all that was good about America. I talked with the fine young men and women who were serving their country so far from home. They were wonderful young kids, all bright and shiny and full of hope and ambition. Being on the ship made the controversy seem less significant. The ship was there and strong, and so were the Navy sailors. I felt like I could tell John that all was well. The ship that was a legacy to him would carry on, and so would his family. I was glad to have my naval son Jack with me, because it was his legacy now, too.

I am in my sixties now. My husband is gone, and my attitude toward the world has changed since I was a young college graduate unsure of my place in the world. For one, I have a new understanding of women's strength. When we stop being scared, when we care more about being powerful than being nice, there is so much we can do.

Former Liberian president Ellen Johnson Sirleaf once told me how she and her colleague Leymah Gbowee organized the country's women in 2003 for a mass action for peace. They led nonviolent protests and declared a sex strike. The basic idea was, "That's it guys. Get your act together. No more sex until you stop fighting." Soon, the war that had been going on for some fourteen years ended, and Sirleaf was elected president. The story made me laugh in absolute joy. These women understood what it would take to pull the country together, and they had the strength to stand up to the men who were tearing it apart.

We need more female leadership in this country, too, and the commonsense approaches it often inspires. Some of my closest friends today are current or former Democratic senators, including Heidi Heitkamp of North Dakota and Amy Klobuchar of Minnesota. I joined both of them on a trip to Central America and Mexico in 2013 on the issue of human trafficking. We spent time with the federal police and state officials and got a fascinating view of the situation. We also became good friends. We didn't agree on everything—they wanted more federal money put into the problem, and I focused more on buy-in from the general public and support from NGOs (nongovernmental organizations). But those kinds of disagreements can be worked out. I also got to know Kamala Harris from California and the two senators from Nevada, Jacky Rosen and Catherine Cortez Masto, all of whom have committed to fight human trafficking. When Catherine was attorney general of Nevada, she oversaw a major effort to break up sex-trafficking rings and helped pass a law to make trafficking illegal in the state. Men can understand these issues, but I have seen that it often takes a woman leader to get action.

I've had people question me about being good friends with Democrats, and I admit it frustrates me every time. My answer is—well, they're my friends. Let's stop at that. I still speak regularly to all of them by phone. I did, however, check with John the first time I wanted to travel with my Democratic friends.

"If this will hurt you in any way, I won't do it," I said.

"No way, and of course you should do it," he said. "In fact, we all should."

I knew that John's friendship with the actor Warren Beatty had surprised some people, too. Though Beatty is known as a left-wing liberal and has always supported Democrats, he and John called each other often and talked freely about politics and ideas. It was a nice relationship and they understood each other. We had known Warren and his wife, Annette Bening, since before they had children. When we had four kids and they did, too, our get-togethers felt like a scene from a Fellini film—utter chaos. But as their kids got older, John showed them around the Capitol, and John and Warren moved a little closer politically. Getting older can shave off some of the rough edges and help you see another viewpoint.

I liked connecting with the women senators who shared my fervor for humanitarian issues, and I appreciated how much they fought for the rights of women and children. We need more women in the Senate and the House. Our convoluted and expensive campaign system makes it harder for women to break into the political networks, but it can be done. Arizona, like Nevada, has been in the forefront of this cause. Whether I support their positions or not, both of our senators are female, and I think that's pretty cool.

I have my own passions on humanitarian causes, but I also know that John expected I would carry on his messages about international leadership and security. He helped turn the 2017 Munich Security Conference into one of the most important foreign policy meetings in the world, and in the final year of his life, he desperately wanted to attend one last time. When it became clear that John was just too ill and couldn't make it, he asked me to go in his place. I didn't want to leave him—but I knew that my being in Munich would be even more important to him. I read the speech on his behalf, honored to be able to speak his words addressing the Syrian refugee crisis and America's need to step up to the plate. Back in our home at Oak Creek, John watched me give the speech on a live stream.

"I was heartbroken not to be there," he said when I got back, "but I'm so proud of what you did."

After that, the Munich conference became as meaningful to me as it had been to John. We need opportunities for world leaders to gather, share ideas, and understand the effect our decisions have on one another. However much we want to stand on our own, we live in an interdependent global world, and closing our eyes to transatlantic issues is counterproductive and naïve. Our security depends on understanding the world situation and playing the correct role in international affairs.

For many years when I traveled, I would see people's eyes light up when they saw an American flag on my sleeve or realized that I was from the United States. We were the ones doing it right. Now people around the world no longer see us as a shining light, and they are often angry that the United States refuses to engage or offer any moral compass to the world. It breaks my heart when I see the ill will now directed toward America, and I hope it will change again. America can be the best of the best again, and if we refuse to step up, then we will watch the wrong players gain more and more influence.

It is easy to become numb to world tragedy. Too often we see the tragic photos from a refugee crisis on the front page of *The New York Times* or watch heartrending images on CNN and we absorb it but don't act on it. I have heard people say that it's too overwhelming so they can't get involved. I encourage them to get involved anyway. They're just the kind of people we need.

I don't think there is any real or meaningful way to analyze all the needs in the world and decide which most deserves your attention. Instead, choose whatever it is that most moves your heart. If you do that, you will wind up in the space where you can do the most good. I believe that passion for a cause always begins with an experience—something you see or smell or encounter in one way or another. It triggers the feeling you just have to do something. It doesn't have to be a huge international issue, either. It can be a change at your local school or volunteering at the food bank. Devote yourself to causes where your emotions are engaged and your heart can lead the way.

When I became a mother for the first time, my outlook on the world changed. All of a sudden, every child in the world could have been my own. I knew how fiercely I tried to protect my babies from harm, and I also came to understand that almost every parent in the world shared that instinct. How tragic when civil war, hunger, or violence prevents you from fulfilling that most basic desire.

In articles written about me over the years, reporters have sometimes complained that I kept my cellphone close and glanced at it often. You bet I did, and I still do. When Jack and Jimmy were deployed in the military, I clutched my phone at all hours, knowing they might have only the briefest window to talk and not wanting to miss any chance. I suppose I also feared getting bad news.

Jimmy called from Iraq one day when we were on the campaign

bus, and after we spoke briefly, John said, "Let me talk to him." Several senators, including Joe Lieberman and Lindsey Graham, were with us that day, and since they all knew Jimmy, John passed along greetings from them. Suddenly the line went dead. We all looked at one another—worried and not knowing what to think. Later, we learned that security at the call center had been monitoring the conversation, and hearing all these high-profile names, suddenly panicked. They shut down the entire call center for twenty-four hours. I felt bad for the Marines who didn't get to make their calls that day, but it didn't change my approach. You would have had to cut my arm off to get my phone from me when they might have been in harm's way. Staying connected to my children is a number one priority.

Now that my children are older and becoming parents themselves, my role has changed—but being available for them still takes precedence over most anything else. We text all the time, and however scattered we are geographically, we stay closely connected by love and emotion. When my children and their spouses began having babies of their own, I sometimes clutched my cellphone for more joyful reasons—awaiting the news of a new grandchild! I don't try to provide advice on parenting, but I am as committed to being available for my children now as I always have been. Being a mom means being there when you are needed. Just listening is enough sometimes.

One day, in the first year after John's death, Jimmy called me from our cabin and began to sob. Opening a closet door, he had found all of John's clothes, and just seeing them had brought back the hurt and sorrow. I understood. I hadn't moved any of John's things yet because facing them was too much for me. In that moment, Jimmy didn't need me to do anything, and I didn't try to provide any counsel other than a loving and understanding ear. One of the things I have learned is that we can give strength by our presence and caring as well as by our words.

It means a lot to have my children around, and I am grateful when that can happen. After the funeral, Jack went right back to Afghanistan, where he was in the midst of his complicated mission of teaching Afghan pilots to fly Black Hawks. With his language skills and flying ability, he was the perfect person for it, but I still breathed a sigh of relief when, after many years of naval service, he returned to the United States. Not long ago, he moved back to Phoenix with his wife, Renee, and their little boy, John S. McCain V, known to all as Mac. I don't know if the Navy is in Mac's future or if he will choose another course entirely. Either is fine. I do know he will inherit a great sense of purpose and service from both his parents. If someday he wants to know more about the legacy extending back with his name, I think he will be very proud.

With all that has happened in my life, I have learned to fight for the changes that matter and look for the good and positive in every situation. When the coronavirus hit America in early 2020 and stay-at-home orders were put in place, my constant travel came to an abrupt halt. I went to the cabin with Jimmy's wife, Holly, and their new baby. Seeing that sweet baby in the place that his grandfather so loved was a joyous reminder of the circle of life. Spots that had held such sad memories for me now resounded with the happy sounds of a baby's laughter. Being at the cabin started to feel comfortable and right again. In this house, we had experienced great wins, great losses, family problems, and family togetherness. We had celebrated firsts, celebrated weddings, and then celebrated the greatest loss of all. Now I understood what John had meant when he said that he wanted his death to be a celebration of a life well lived. If you fill each day with meaning, purpose, service, family, and love, you never have cause to mourn.

On what would have been our fortieth wedding anniversary, I talked to my family, hugged my grandbaby, and thought about how full my life had been since the day I met a handsome naval officer in

Hawaii. Our years together were a great gift. I loved John and missed him so much, but I was proud to be staying strong for our children, our grandchildren, and our country. I felt a surge of sadness not to have John at my side, but also great happiness for all we had experienced together. So many possibilities still remained ahead, and there was pleasure to be had in each day. As I walked outside around his beloved cabin in northern Arizona, the sun was shining, the grass was green, and the birds were singing. I wanted to tell John all about it. But somehow, I think he already knew.

ACKNOWLEDGMENTS

It has been a pleasure to work on this book with the support of so many gifted people. Thanks to editor Mary Reynics and the strong team at Crown Forum, including Tina Constable, Campbell Wharton, Derek Reed, Emily Hartley, Susan Corcoran, Cindy Murray, and Jessalyn Foggy. Very warm thanks also to Byrd Leavell and David Buchalter at UTA, who believed in this book from the start.

I am grateful to writer Janice Kaplan for bringing my words to the page with such grace and energy. I appreciate her insights and her talent at crafting my many experiences into a compelling narrative. Our collaboration has been wonderfully creative and inspiring.

Meghan Latcovitch is officially my chief of staff but is truly my rock—the person I trust to see me through many situations. Long-time McCainiacs Rick Davis, Mark Salter, and Carla Eudy are good friends and valued advisers and I appreciate our continued connection. Sharon and Oliver Harper gave me courage in the final days of John's life, staying resolutely at my side, and I will never forget their strength and kindness.

I tell many stories about my children in this book, and I am so proud of the adults they have become. Jack and Jimmy are amazing patriots and fine young men. Meghan and Bridget are genuinely loving, caring, and supportive. The wonderful spouses they have chosen strengthen our family and enrich my life.

I am thankful to have such darling grandchildren, and I hope when they get bigger, they will read this book and understand more about me and their family. I want them to know that politics can be in the service of good and that serving your country with honor is an ideal not to be forgotten.

Finally to John, my love of four decades. You are my inspiration always. Ours was a great partnership. I loved being by your side—and thank you for teaching me about bravery so that I can stand alone now and flourish.

PHOTOGRAPH CREDITS

———⤬⤬⤬———

1 Cindy, with John in Navy uniform: courtesy of the author

2 (*top*) Cindy and John wedding portrait: Updike Photography

2 (*bottom*) John and Cindy honeymoon in Hawaii: courtesy of the author

3 (*top*) Cindy crowned Junior Rodeo Queen: Arizona Republic/USA TODAY NETWORK

3 (*bottom*) Cindy with sorority sisters: courtesy of the author

4 (*top*) Cindy and her father: courtesy of the author

4 (*bottom*) Three generations of McCains: courtesy of the author

5 (*top*) Roberta McCain: Jeff Kida

5 (*bottom*) Cindy and her plane: Martha Morris

6 (*top*) McCains with their children during Senate run: courtesy of the author

6 (*bottom*) McCains with their children on the Capitol steps: courtesy of the author

7 (*top*) John McCain with Walter Cronkite: CBS Photo Archive/Getty Images

7 (*bottom*) Cindy in Bangladesh orphanage: courtesy of the author

8 McCain family during 2000 presidential campaign: McCain Campaign

9 (*top*) McCain family at Arizona ranch: Ken Akers Photography

9 (*bottom*) Cindy, John, and Jack (with midshipman's cap): courtesy of the author

10 (*top*) Jimmy leaving for Camp Pendleton: courtesy of the author

10 (*bottom*) Jack and John in their flight jackets: courtesy of the author

11 Cindy and Bridget: AP Photo/Jae C. Hong

12 (*top*) Cindy with Mother Teresa: courtesy of the author

12 (*bottom*) Cindy with racing car: N. Scott Trimble/USA TODAY
NETWORK

13 (*top*) Cindy with Iraqi family: Ken Akers Photography

13 (*bottom*) Cindy in the Democratic Republic of Congo: Meghan Latcovich

14 (*top*) Cindy visiting refugee camp, seated, with child: Meghan Latcovich

14 (*bottom*) Cindy speaking with people in crowd: Meghan Latcovich

15 Joe Biden speaking at John McCain's funeral: David Hume Kennerly/
Center for Creative Photography/University of Arizona

16 Jack and Renee's wedding, family portrait: Chrisman Studios

ABOUT THE AUTHOR

CINDY McCAIN is the chairman of the board of the McCain Institute for International Leadership. Married to Senator John McCain for thirty-eight years, Cindy became well known for her support of military families and for her speech at the 2008 Republican National Convention that nominated John as the party's presidential candidate. She is chairman of her family business, Hensley Beverage Co., and her extensive philanthropic and humanitarian work has won her many awards. Cindy and John raised four children together: Meghan, Jimmy, Jack, and Bridget. Cindy now travels extensively to raise awareness of human trafficking around the world, but her home base remains in Phoenix, Arizona.

Twitter: @cindymccain